Mulroy
Bay
Ranny
Woodquarter
Cratlagh
Gortnavern
Lough
Ballyboe
Lough
Nacally
Ross
Point
Tirhoman
Garrygort
Kilwarry
Lough Columbkille
snant
MILFORD
Claggan
Lough Doo
tmacall
Loughras
Glebe
Ballyconnell
New Town
Forquar
Moyle
Long Hill
Thorn
Lough
Carn High
Clooney
ough Fern
Carn Low
To Ramelton

Buchanan   *Buchanan*

Loch Lomond

In search of Buchanan

'Clarior hinc honos'

The stories of some Buchanan ancestors before and after the emigration of James Buchanan of Ramelton, County Donegal, Ireland, in 1783.

Some of these stories are incorporated in the BBC1 TV documentary -

'Are you related to an American President?'
- produced by Big Mountain Productions.

Irene Martin

Rossnashannagh Publishing 2011

Copyright © Irene Martin 2011

The right of Irene Martin to be identified as the author and designer of this work has been asserted in accordance with the Copyright, Designs and Patents Act, 1988.

Published by Rossnashannagh Publishing.

www.insearchofbuchanan.com

All rights reserved. No part of this publication may be reproduced, stored in a retrieval system, or transmitted in any form or by any means electronic, mechanical, photocopying, recording or otherwise without the prior written permission of the copyright owners and the publisher.

Printed by: Browne Printers, Letterkenny Tel: +353 (0) 74 91 21387

ISBN: 978-0-9567979-0-2   In Search of Buchanan   Paperback

Front Cover Illustration: Portrait of James Buchanan by Richard Ainsworth.

Landscape of County Donegal Thatched Cottage by Raymond Cochrane.

Back Cover Photograph: Great grandparents Samuel Buchanan and Rebecca Cheatley on their wedding day. (Known as "White Sam" when he was older, born 1836 and died 9 July 1920 age 84.)

CONTENTS

                                                                                          Page

Acknowledgements   i

Dedication

Introduction   1

Chapter 1   Anselan   5

His emigration from Roe Valley, Limavady in Ulster, to Scotland. - How Anselan's clan prospered in Scotland - Networking through marriage - Neighbourhood networks - The search for Buchanan of Gartincaber - The search for Buchanan of Blairlusk - Evidence of the Buchanan colonial spread 1016 –1674 in The Lennox, Scotland.

Chapter 2   George   39

Buchanans in the Plantation of Ulster 1609 -1625 – George Buchanan's emigration to Ireland in 1674 - The journey – the landing place at Bready on the River Foyle - Buchanan burials in Grange graveyard near Bready - Buchanan burials in Termonmagurk Parish in County Tyrone - Deroran - the Lowry (Belmore) and Buchanan connection in Finagh Manor.

Chapter 3   Thomas   68

Migration from Deroran, County Tyrone to Ramelton in County Donegal – the port – the linen industry – the community – the Presbyterians and Covenanters – Francis Makemie 1683 - the linen trade.

Chapter 4   James

The birthplace of James Buchanan, Ramelton – his Russell grandparents' place at Stony Batter, south of Ramelton where he was reared – the search for Buchanan in Hearth Money Rolls in 1662, Buchanan freeholders 1761 – the search in Griffiths Valuation of land for Buchanan occupants 1848 – Ramelton Church Records – James Buchanan's emigration to America 1783 on board the ship *Providence* that sailed from Derry – Arrived in Philadelphia and met by Uncle Joshua Russell   - Journey to Gettysburg on horseback with Uncle Joshua - Working at Russell's Tavern - Russell and Buchanan gravestones in Black's Graveyard -   Land Warrants in Pennsylvania - Donegal Presbyterian Church - Lower Marsh Creek Presbyterian Church - John Tom and Cove Gap Trading Post near Mercersburg, bought and renamed 'Stony Batter' by James Buchanan - Dunwoodie Farm purchased - Spring Grove Cemetery - James Buchanan's gravestone - The birthplace of President James Buchanan in 1791 - Emigrant letter from James Edward Buchanan, Texas, to the Presbyterian minister in Ramelton - shared ancestry with the President.

Appendix I: Marriages
Appendix II: Wills and Testaments
Appendix III: The Killing Times
Appendix IV: Sasines of Lands in Scotland 1461 - 1515
Appendix V: Muster Rolls 1630, Ireland
Appendix VI: Church of Ireland Records
Appendix VII: Flax growers lists 1796
Appendix VIII: Civil Survey 1655 Parish of Raphoe
Appendix IX: Inquisitions of Ulster, Donegal
Appendix X: Hearth Money Rolls 1662

Bibliography

Abbreviations:

COI Church of Ireland, MIC Microfilm, NAI National Archives of Ireland, NLI National Library Ireland, PRONI Public Record Office of Northern Ireland.

Acknowledgements

My sincere thanks go to Dr. Patrick Fitzgerald and Dr. John Lynch for their enthusiastic and inspirational encouragement to persevere in my research - in what sometimes felt an overwhelming task.

I also wish to acknowledge the faithful support I received from Mrs. Christine Johnston, senior library assistant in the Centre for Migration Studies, Omagh.

For access to the voluminous Buchanan research in the Ulster American Folk Park, Omagh, that was kindly and freely made available to me - my grateful thanks to Mr. Frank Collins.

For his very generous hospitality, and for sharing his wealth of knowledge related to the USA Buchanan immigrants, to Mr. Kevin Shue of Lancaster Historical Society, Pennsylvania, USA, I owe my heartfelt thanks.

My thanks also go to Mrs. Freda McKelvey and her son, for the visit to her family home, Deroran House, County Tyrone, ancestral home of Thomas Buchanan, Ramelton, the ancestor of President James Buchanan, and for her gracious hospitality on the occasion of our visit and permission to take photographs.

To Mrs. Sarah Ferguson (née Buchanan) last surviving Buchanan of an older generation at the High Carn, Ramelton, Co Donegal, for granting me a wonderful interview which helped to corroborate information from a hitherto unknown line of the family – sincere thanks.

To Mrs. Carol Hemfrey, of Drymen, Scotland, a retired Chartered Town Planner and specialist in Conservation, an Elder in Drymen Parish Church, a founder Member of the Drymen and District Local History Society, a founder Member of Drymen Heritage Local Community Development Trust, and an ex Tourist Information Officer, for her approaches to the various owners of previously owned Scottish Buchanan farms and estates on my behalf, and for accompanying me on the subsequent visits, my very sincere thanks. Also for the various items of research located and information provided, these are greatly appreciated.

My thanks to the staff in:

Northern Ireland:	PRONI, Belfast; the webmaster at Bready Ancestry, Tyrone; Ballymena Library, Coleraine Library and Omagh Library.
Republic of Ireland:	Donegal Ancestry, Ramelton, Co Donegal; National Archives, Dublin; Court House Archives in Lifford, Co Donegal.
Scotland:	Mitchell Library in Glasgow, Map Archives; Stirling University Library Archives; Dumfries Library; Dumfries Historical Archives; Stranraer Library; Drymen Library; Dunbartonshire Council Archives and Dumbarton Library.
U. S. A.	Franklin and Marshall College Archives, Lancaster, Pennsylvania; Historical Society archives in Gettysburg, York, Philadelphia and Lancaster. 'Wheatland', the President James Buchanan ancestral home, Lancaster; Mercersburg Library Archives – the James Buchanan Collection. Pensylvania State Archives, Harrisburg.

To the ministers and members of the congregations of the Presbyterian churches of Drymen and Kilmaronock in Scotland; Ramelton in Co. Donegal, Ireland; Donegal Presbyterian Church in Lancaster County, U.S.A; Lower Marsh Creek Presbyterian Church in Chambersburg County, U.S.A; for their kind assistance - my sincere thanks.

To my late father, to my mother, brother, sister and to members of my extended family, thank you for permitting me to quiz you in my interviews. Thanks also to Margie, Kathy, Eleanor and Jean for the craíc* during our Buchanan reunions. Special thanks to my two daughters, Paula and Sophie, and sister Anne, for draft proof reading, and support.

For final proof reading and help in my first venture into publishing and print I thank Willie Patterson, Bob Tate, Willi Barton, Kevin Shue and Carol Hemfrey. Your assistance is greatly appreciated. I thank my son-in-law Keith Irwin who constructed a brilliant website for the book called 'insearchofbuchanan.com'. I thank my son Graham for facilitating and upgrading me with the latest in 'state-of-the-art' telecommunication hardware for my many travels.

Last, but not least, to my husband, Jimmy, for his love, patience, and unswerving support in accompanying me on my fact-finding expeditions to Counties Donegal and Tyrone in Ireland, and to Scotland and America. Amongst the many miles travelled as campervan driver and companion, many fond memories are of him gently scraping the moss from the ancient monuments and gravestones. Your patience is legendary. Most importantly, thanks for agreeing to permanently migrate to Ireland from the Isle of Man, thus facilitating my desire to take the Queen's University of Belfast Master of Social Science Degree in Irish Migration Studies, which I was awarded with commendation in 2009.

Every effort has been made to trace and contact copyright holders before publication. Any errors or omissions will be rectified by the publisher at the earliest opportunity, if notified. My thanks to all who have given permission to publish copyright material.

- *A Word used in Ireland to describe great enjoyment, fun and laughter where folks are gathered.*

County Donegal Cottages, Ireland   by Raymond Cochrane

This work is dedicated to

my aunt Rae Wilson

'Keeper of the Family Archives'

1917 - 1989

INTRODUCTION

'That is why we tell stories, so that they can be with us always'.

In 1989 my story-telling aunt died. She was my father's sister. Not only was she a wife, mother, grandmother, sister and aunt, she was our family's 'Keeper of the Family Archives'.

As 'Keeper of the Archives' her stories were mostly anecdotal, and the people in the stories were identifiable in the family tree she had made, which dated back a long way. She was a busy farmer's wife. Scribbled notes were made on the backs of envelopes and scraps of paper, and in no particular order, as she came across important information. A few emigrant letters survived the bonfires of the newly married wives who had joined the family down through the years.

A Family Bible where names and dates had been recorded was among a drawer full of sources, along with bits and pieces of extracts from various newspapers, and numerous well thumbed letters containing responses to her far-flung queries. There were also faded sepia photographs and other ancient archival documentation.

In a time when travel was expensive and home internet was non-existent, her research activities by letter were impeded. She came to a point where she could not progress her research. According to family tradition our family had migrated from Blairlusk, Gartocharn, Loch Lomond, Scotland, to Ulster, Ireland, in 1674. She knew this but could find no evidence to verify it.

She knew from the ancestral stories that they had migrated from a farm in the Loch Lomond area called Blairlusk. However, according to her Scottish sources, Blairlusk did not exist in any Scottish map of that 17th century, nor in the 18th century, nor in the 1960s. I was given her research collection before she died, and in due course I began to make my own investigations into the stories.

I was unprepared for the shocking revelations that emerged, and totally unprepared for my involvement in a television production for the BBC in 2010 related to my amazing story. Following the promise that I had made to my aunt concerning the search for Blairlusk, the first challenge for me was to find the evidence. The top priority for me was the need to establish that these were true accounts of real people, who lived, breathed and had shared my DNA with a common ancestor.

The second challenge was to locate and read all the published research associated with these times and places, the people who lived there and then, and their previous and subsequent migrations.

The third challenge was to link up all the orally communicated traditional stories of connections in this Buchanan diaspora and to make visits to the various migration locations of the Buchanan homestead at Blairlusk, Loch Lomond, Scotland; the Buchanan homestead at Carn, north of Ramelton; Stony Batter, which was the homestead of James Buchanan's Russell grandparents south of Ramelton in County Donegal,

Ireland; Russell's Tavern near Gettysburg; Stony Batter, the Buchanan trading post in Cove Gap, Pennsylvania – named after the old Russell homestead back in County Donegal, and 'Wheatland' the home of President James Buchanan in Lancaster, Pennsylvania.

The 'Keeper of the Archives' was Rae Wilson, and she was the grand-daughter of 'White' Sam Buchanan of Garrygort, Milford, County Donegal, Ulster – my great grandfather, who was also a nephew of James Buchanan who was President of the USA from 1857 – 1861.

'White' Sam Buchanan was the son of John Buchanan and Martha McNutt. They had met Ambassador James Buchanan, in 1833, when he came visiting his cousins at the Cairn (Carn), Ramelton, enquiring about his father's birth certificate and records concerning his ancestry as he intended to run for President of the United States of America in future years.

At the time of his visit to Ramelton he was the American Ambassador to Russia and he was on his way home from Russia. Ambassador James Buchanan's letter dated 1833 tells of his trip from Liverpool to Donegal, where he found that "the women were delightful", and the "hot toddy" was quite something to be experienced. After his visit Martha Buchanan entered into correspondence with their Uncle James Buchanan on the issue of slavery in America. These letters have not yet been located, but are recollected in oral family tradition.

My search began, and I was able to augment my aunt's findings with rich new pickings over the many miles travelled and many choice nuggets unearthed in the various locations of primary source material linking Scotland, Ireland and the United States of America. What I was looking for were private letters, newspapers of the time, diaries and journals, voices from the past. I wanted those people to come visually alive again in the artistic richness of colour, tone, texture, pattern and dimension of the era in which they lived. I was not disappointed. This is my story.

The following ancestors are descendants of Anselan O'Cahan (O'Kyan) from the Roe Valley near Limavady circa 1016, who link down through history to my family via the Buchanan family tree from Scotland.

Anselan O' Kyan, who emigrated from Ireland to Scotland in 1016.

George Buchanan, Anselan's descendant, who migrated from Scotland to Ireland in 1674.

Thomas Buchanan, internal migrant from County Tyrone to County Donegal circa 1700 and who emigrated to Pennsylvania in the mid 18th century.

James Buchanan, who emigrated from County Donegal to Pennsylvania, in 1783 at the end of the American Revolution.

My aim in writing this book was to be able to widen the perception of, and gain some insight into, Irish migration and socialisation rather than to depend on a narrower concept of diaspora, through the study of the individual migrant's decisions and choices as reflected in their diasporic footprint. I hoped to be able to respond to the issues of home, identity, religious and economic opportunities, and networks, as part of the ongoing debate on Irish migration. These Buchanan migrants are part of that story.

The evidence gathered for my book was based on the data and accounts from my research, investigation, and visits to migrants' actual locations, which may inform us as to why there was a Buchanan diaspora in Scotland, Ireland and America in the 17th and 18th centuries.

My premise is that a vital constituent of their migration was their Presbyterian form of their Christian faith, their covenant with God, their weekly Sabbath networking, more than any other component that underpinned their decision to move. This supported their desire for economic betterment. I endeavoured to validate this premise by research from Church records.

What was of great importance for me in this research was the opportunity, as never before in history, of accessing so much relevant and excellent resources online. The resources are endless in terms of accessing maps, public records, national archives and out-of-print publications which have now been digitalised and are available online.

Visiting locations online in America and Scotland to plan the expedition routes facilitated the travel arrangements. Booking the campervan via the internet to follow the Buchanan migrant trail in America that I had devised online was easy. Paying for the travel in advance was possible through the use of credit and debit cards, reducing the need to carry cash. Other technology included having a camera in a mobile phone, convenient at a moment's notice, to record gravestones for example. Using a scanner to copy items on to the computer to make different forms of records was very expedient. Photocopies were very useful records of information from historical deposits in various archive locations, relieving the tedious chore of hand writing copies.

There is nothing to compare with actually being there, where the migrant lived, travelled, worked and worshipped. The images, (for example the Allegheny Mountains), the smells (for example peat, turf and wood smoke), the tastes (for example pumpkin pie), talking to the people, and travelling through the landscape all contributed to the experience of the hands-on migration of these Buchanans.

Speaking to older people who lived in the area, who knew, or knew of, the person or family, or speaking to descendants or other family connections also provided a much more real and tangible life picture of the migrant and his or her life and times.

Visits to places like the Ulster American Folk Park at Omagh, Penn's Landing in Philadelphia, Clarinch island in Loch Lomond, Scotland, and the ruined dwelling at 'Stony Batter' at Ramelton, County Donegal, evoked the past in more than feelings of nostalgia. These were the places called 'home' belonging to the migrants. By this I mean that the sense of living history, being able to identify with the migrants in their movements, and empathising with their life and times, felt almost like being in a time warp.

When I saw the log cabin in Pennsylvania called 'Stony Batter' – named after the thatched cottage back home in Ramelton that James Buchanan remembered in his mind's eye, the impact of what I was witnessing was somewhat overwhelming and emotional for me. This was his home from home. When I eventually found the grave of this James Buchanan who emigrated from Ireland in 1783, I experienced this same reaction as I learned of his tragic unexpected death.

These visits enabled me to enter in, and inhabit, the migrant's world for a moment in time. I begin the selected Buchanan migrants' stories with Anselan who migrated in 1016 from Ireland to Scotland.

Illustration 1 Rae, the keeper of the Archives
Illustration 2 'White' Sam Buchanan and Rebecca Cheatley

Chapter 1   ANSELAN

> San Antonio, Texas.
> May 14/97.
>
> Reverend and Dear Sir:
>
> Through the courtesy of Mr Alex Mitchell who has kindly given me other information upon the subject under enquiry, I have been given your address with belief expressed that you would not be unwilling to aid me. It is my desire to secure what information is obtainable of my ancestors who reside in your County and were possibly members of your Church. About the middle of the 16th century George Buchanan of Blairlusk in Scotland who was the decendant of the renox of Walter 13th Laird of Buchanan sold Blairlusk to his brother William

ANSELAN

This portion of the scroll of the Buchanan family tree shows Anselan, born circa 980 AD.

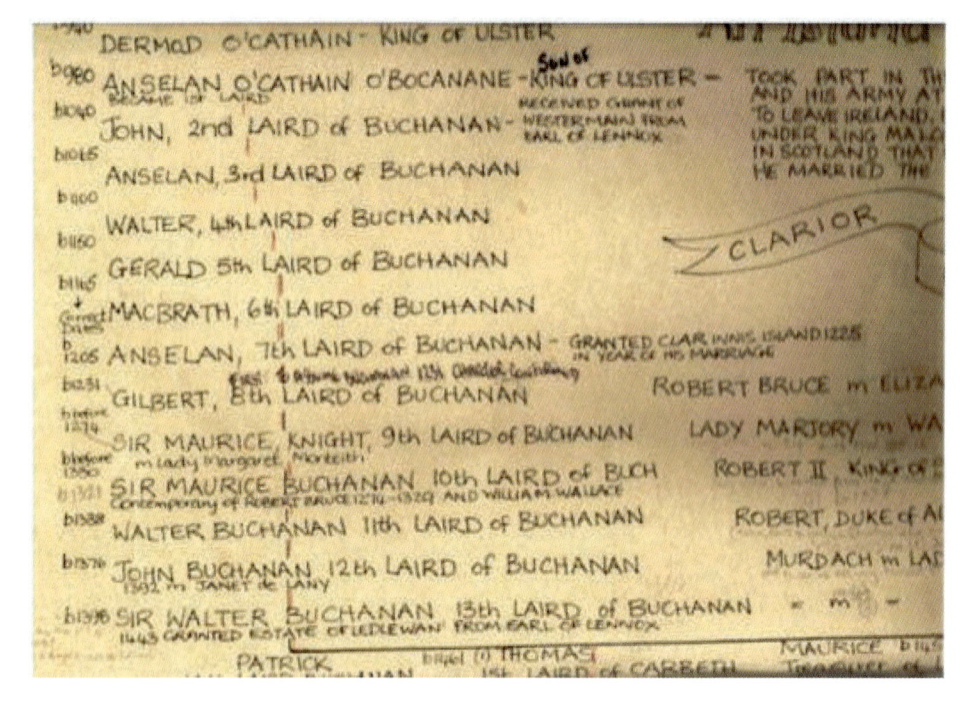

Illustration 3   Taken from a family scroll in possession of the author.

ANSELAN O'CAHAN (O'Kyan, O'Boquahanne or anglicised Buchanan.)
  The first source states that after seven centuries of raiding, the Danes, under 'Swein the Fork-Beard' took control of most of England and Ireland in 1013 and 1014. His son, Canute (994-1035) was then crowned King of England.[1]

  Swein ordered celebrations which were to be held in the Garrison at Limerick, Ireland, and instructions were given for daughters of the Irish nobility to be present. Fergussin was the Danish General in charge of the garrison, the feast and celebrations. Instead, a number of Irish youths from Ulster were dispatched, disguised in women's habits, with long Irish scains (daggers) concealed below their cloaks. A massacre of the Danes followed. The leader of these youths was Anselan Buey O'Kyan, or O'Cahan, son of the King of the West Part of Ulster.

Map 1   Location of O'Cahan lands in Ireland before the Normans, c1100.

(Ua Catháin, Ciannachta)[2]

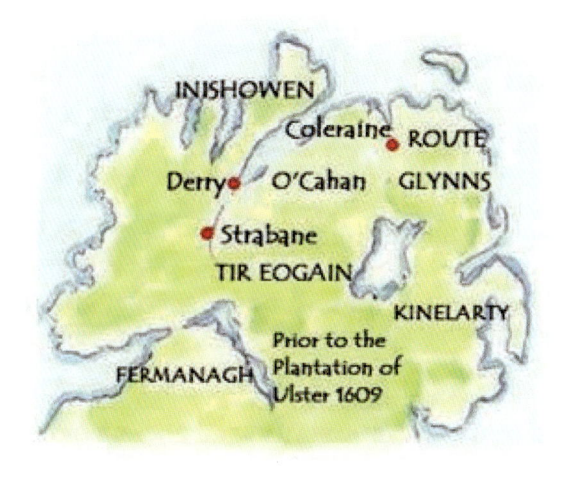

Map 2   O'Cahan lands prior to the Plantation of Ulster 1609.

O'Cahan lands were confiscated during the Plantation of Ulster – Manus O'Cahan received some of his land back as a deserving Irishman.

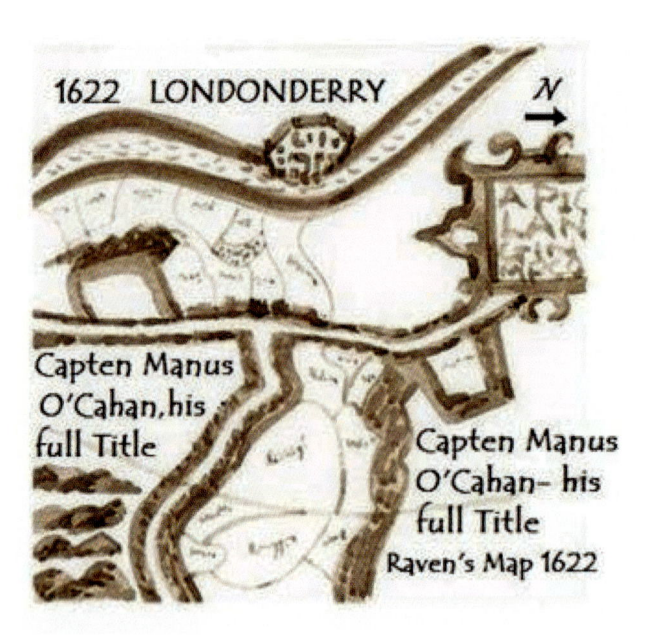

Map 3   Information from Raven's Map: 'A Plat of the Lands belonging to the Company of Goldsmiths 1622'. [3]

This map confirms that there had been O'Cahans who owned lands in this area prior to the 17th century. This was also Anselan O'Cahan's territory.

O'Cahans of Drenagh, Limavady.[4]

    The second source states that the anglicised family name McCausland (son of Auselan – derived from Anselan) goes back more than 900 years to an O'Cahan named Anselan, son of Kyan, King of Ulster. Anselan was forced to leave Ireland in about 1016 on account of his share in a 'memorable stratagem where he and other young Irishmen dressed in women's attire surprised and slaughtered their Danish oppressors'. When Malcolm II of Scotland heard of Anselan's feats he invited him to become his Master of Arms and 'bestowed ample lands upon him in The Lennox'.

    This is linked with a third source which states that in 1016, with a price on his head, Anselan fled from Ireland and emigrated to Scotland. Eventually he acquired lands in The Lennox, both by marriage and as a reward for winning battles, for services rendered to King Malcolm II of Scotland (1005-1034). The Lennox was broadly known to extend from Loch Lomond in the west to Stirling in the east. In addition, Anselan was granted Arms practically identical to those used by the Buchanan Society of Scotland today.[5] Therefore records do exist of an 'Anselan'.

Illustration 4 shows the evidence that King Malcolm II was the reigning monarch in Scotland at the time of Anselan's migration from Ireland after the Battle of Limerick 1016.[6]

THE KINGS OF SCOTLAND
House of Alpin

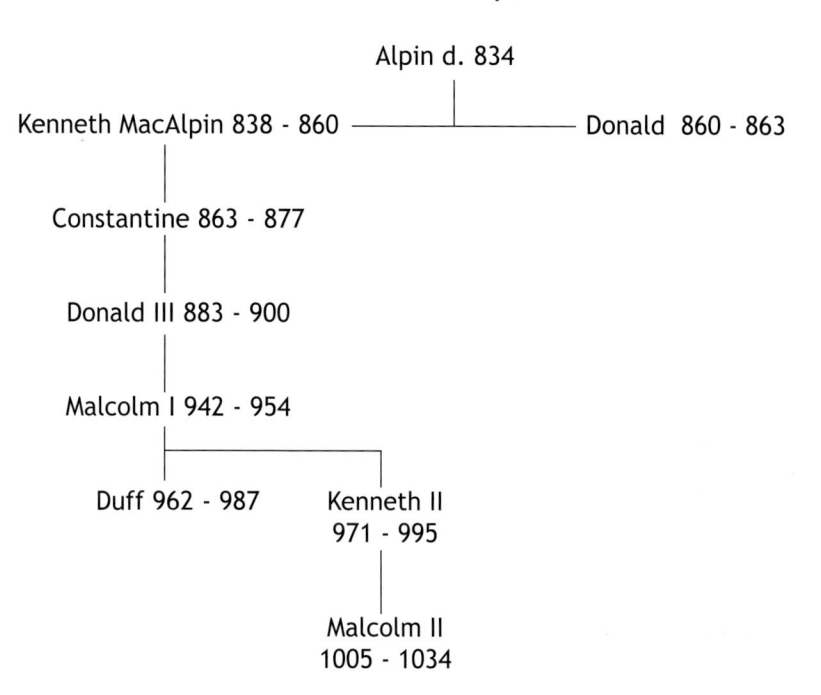

```
                    Alpin d. 834
                         |
Kenneth MacAlpin 838 - 860 ──┴── Donald 860 - 863
         |
Constantine 863 - 877
         |
Donald III 883 - 900
         |
Malcolm I 942 - 954
         |
   ┌─────┴─────┐
Duff 962 - 987   Kenneth II
                 971 - 995
                     |
                 Malcolm II
                 1005 - 1034
```

Illustration 4   Lineage of King Malcolm II of Scotland.

Evidence that King Canute was the reigning monarch in England at the time of Anselan's migration from Ireland to Scotland in 1016.[7]

House of Denmark

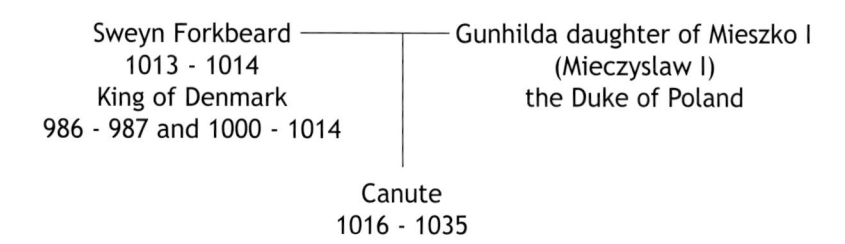

```
Sweyn Forkbeard ──────┬────── Gunhilda daughter of Mieszko I
   1013 - 1014        |           (Mieczyslaw I)
  King of Denmark     |          the Duke of Poland
986 - 987 and 1000 - 1014
                      |
                   Canute
                  1016 - 1035
```

Illustration 5   Lineage of King Canute, the Danish king who conquered England.

This evidence set a strong foundation for the Buchanan migration trail. King Canute had outlawed Anselan in Ireland, and King Malcolm II had welcomed him in Scotland. The migration story in Scotland begins. The main source, William Buchanan of Auchmar, first establishes the Buchanan pedigree as follows:

Anselan Buey, or Fair, was the son of Kyan, provincial king of the west part of Ulster. Anselan O'Kyan left Ireland in the year 1016, the 12th year of King Malcolm II of Scotland, and landed with some attendants upon the northern coast of Argyllshire, near The Lennox.

> 'A nobleman who had a considerable interest in those parts, and in the king's favours, introduced him to the king, who took him into his service against the Danes'.[8]

For his service Anselan acquired the Church lands of Boquanan on Loch Lomond east side, and his descendants took the name O'Boquanan.[9]

The following passage from Auchmar is central to the Buchanan link:

> 'Anselan, the third of that name, born 1205, and seventh laird of Buchanan, who is ordinarily termed, in any record in which he is mentioned, Anselan son of MacBeath, and Sennescallus, or Chamberlain to the Earl of Lennox, in written mortifications, in the Chartulary of the Abbey of Paisley. This Anselan the third, with Gilbert and Methlen, his two sons, are inserted as witnesses in a charter granted by Malduin, Earl of Lennox to Gilmore, son of Maoldonich, of the lands of Luss, in the beginning of the reign of King Alexander the Second and they are called the Earl's clients. Gilbert, Anselan the third's eldest son, and successor, first assumed the surname of Buchanan.'[10]

A fourth source also confirms the existence of Anselan, and that he was awarded lands on the east shore of Loch Lomond for his military services to King Malcolm II. The same source states that over the next two and a half centuries the family name used by Chiefs of Anselan's Clan was MacAuselan (sons of Anselan). It was not until 1240, when Gillebrid (Gilbert) who was seneschal (medieval steward of a great house) to the Earl of Lennox, began to use the name 'de Bucannan', in reference to the name of the territory acquired by the family which was called 'Buchanne' or 'Boquanane'.

As late as 1370, the charter to the land was granted to 'Sir Maurice MacAuselan, Laird of Buchanan.' It was Maurice's grandson who would finally adopt the surname 'Buchanan'.[11]

LOCATION OF THE LENNOX LANDS

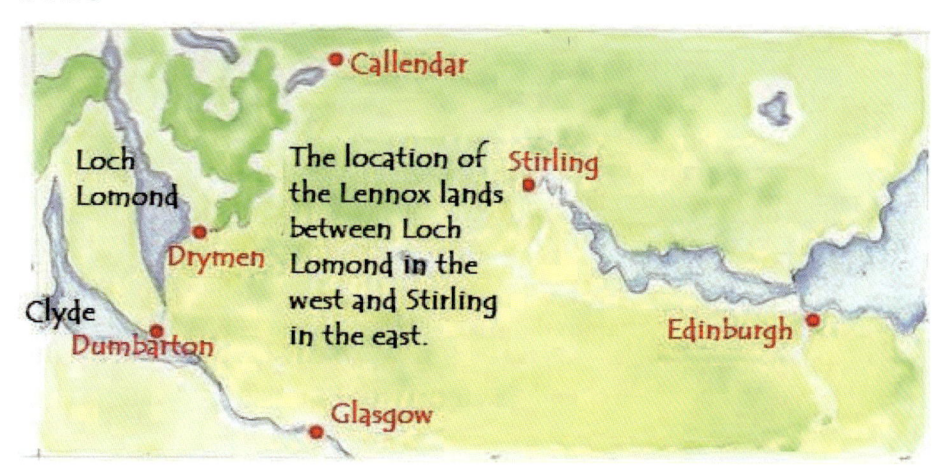

Map 4   Location of the Lennox lands in Scotland – awarded to Anselan and his descendants.

These accounts are similar but it is noticeable that in one account Anselan 'flees' to Scotland while in the other account Anselan is 'invited' by King Malcolm of Scotland to come to Scotland. It depends on the perspective as to whether Anselan became an exile, as described in Miller's *Emigrants and Exiles*, 'emigration remained forced banishment'[12] or that Anselan was a migrant who came to some conclusions and was enticed to move home, and left by choice, 'weighed the alternatives...willed and survived...and ultimately his descendants prospered.'[13]

Anselan's new place called 'home' was in 'The Lennox' or in Gaelic 'Leamhnachd'.[14] These Lennox lands were the location of the networks of the Stewarts and Buchanans. They were the outgrowth of the old Celtic Earldom of Lennox, in the southernmost highlands comprised of what today is Dunbartonshire, a large part of Stirlingshire, and parts of Perthshire and Renfrewshire.

Matthew Stewart, 13th Earl of Lennox, was father of Henry, Lord Darnley, the second husband of Mary Queen of Scots. This Henry Stewart, Lord Darnley, was the father of James VI of Scotland and I of England. The Stewarts and the Buchanans were linked through marriage and kinship.

> 'As Lennox territory Drymen was associated with the Buchanans of Drumakill, who developed Drymen as a market town. By an Act of the Scottish Parliament of 1669, William Buchanan was authorised to have a weekly market on Thursday and two annual fairs on the 10th May and 15th October.' [15]

This demonstrates that the Buchanans were in the land networks of the Lennox (Stewart) families, who were in turn relatives of King James VI (Stewart / Stuart). Buchanans were also married into these Stewart families.

HOW ANSELAN'S CLAN PROSPERED - Chain and Internal Step Migration

These land networks or estates were located around the Great Houses of the landed families. For example there was the Old Buchanan House, known as the 'Place' of Buchanan. The listed buildings of Buchanan include the entry:

> 'Remains of Buchanan old house dated about 1600. The accepted definition of the term "place" is "a main residence and auxiliary buildings grouped round a courtyard or barmkin" '.[16]

There had been Buchanans in possession of these lands for approximately seven hundred years, up to 1682, with certain documentary records going back to 1225.

How can these Lennox lands be described? Are they simply a geographical location with no reference to the people who populated them, or no reference to the migrant movements into and out of, and within these spaces? How could this group of people, or migrants be described? Are they a clan? Are they a colony? Are they part of a 'colonial' spread?

The compromise I have made is that I want to use this term 'colony' to describe, as the dictionary puts it,

> 'a body of people settled in a new territory, retaining ties with their motherland; the body of descendants of settlers wholly or partially retaining their ideology and organisation; rather like a distinguishable localised population within a species (as a community of bees)'.[17]

The land networks or 'colonial spread' is an idea which originated in Sweden and was described by Philip Robinson.[18] This was noted by Fitzgerald and Lambkin.[19] It is certainly applicable in the case of Anselan and his retinue, after their migration to Scotland, if viewed in this context. In fact the history of that whole area is about the spread of this Buchanan 'colony' or clan. The Buchanan 'colonial spread' was from the east coast of Loch Lomond eastwards towards Stirling, northwards towards Callander in the Trossachs, and south-westwards towards Glasgow in the area termed 'The Lennox'.

Thus there is this evidence that the same patterns were established in this area of Scotland long before they were later established in the 'colonisation' during the Plantation of Ulster. This statement of Fitzgerald and Lambkin could have easily applied to the Lennox in earlier times –

> 'the rich, fertile river valleys served as migrant corridors for substantial and permanent penetration of the...interior' [20]

The Endrick, Blane, Dualt, Catter, Kelty Rivers and burns (tributaries) fed this area, and the various locations of the Buchanan settlements would confirm that this spread along the valleys was indeed the case. Lands were acquired and in a later chapter the similarity about the patterns of the Plantation of Ulster settlements is compared.

In 1040 John of Buchanan, 2nd Laird Buchanan, son of Anselan, received the grant of land from the Earl of Lennox called 'Westermains' at Drymen.

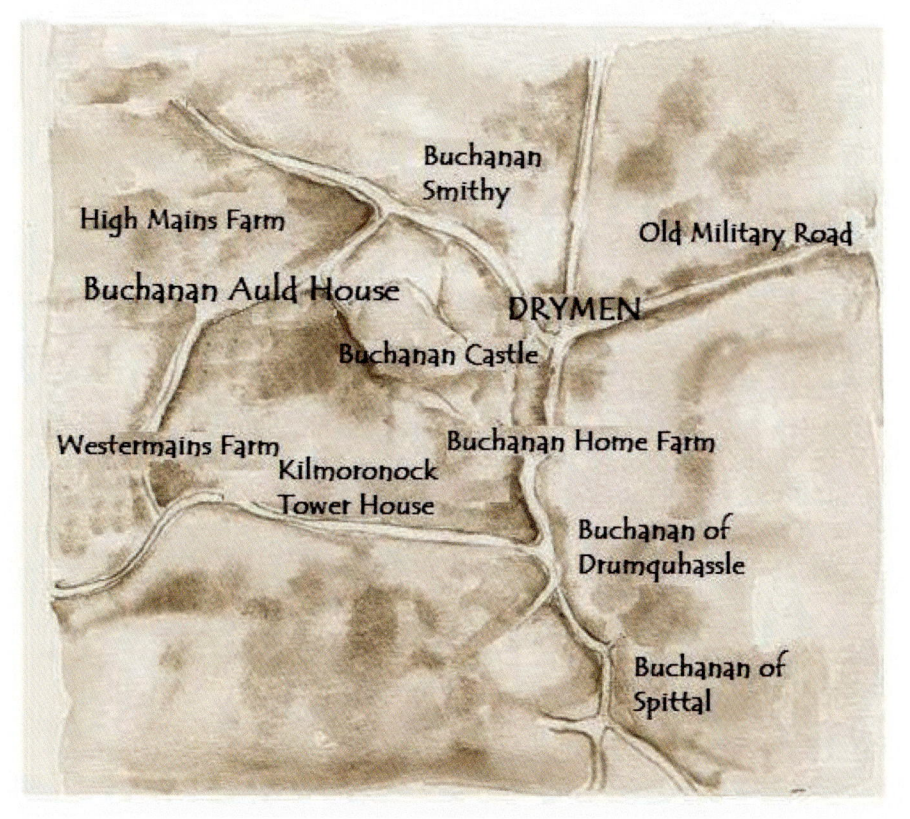

Map 5   Westermains, Drumquhassle and Spittal estates, and Buchanan Auld House and Castle.

The earliest members of the Clan Buchanan were settled on the shores of Loch Lomond where lands were granted by one of the powerful Celtic Earls of Lennox, to Anselan and his son John.

Illustration 6   Clarinch Island opposite Balmaha, east shore of Loch Lomond.

In 1225 Anselan, 7th Laird of Buchanan, was granted Clarinch Island. Other evidence is recorded for lands near Kippen.

'In addition to the 1270 charter for Drumquhassle, a 14th century charter from Robert the Bruce for Boquhan, (Buchanan) near Kippen in Stirlingshire is mentioned on two Great Seal rolls'.[21]

By 1282 Maurice of Buchanan received a renewed charter that granted the lands of Buchanan with baronial rights from the 6th Earl of Lennox; this was a time when feudalism was rapidly developing in Scotland after the influence of the Norman Conquest.

Illustration 7   Buchanan Place – From a Drawing by J. P. Neale, engraved by M.J.Barenger, 1787.

Buchanan Place, also known as Buchanan Auld House, is the site of the ancient seat of the Buchanans. When John Buchanan, the 22nd and the last laird of Buchanan died without heirs in 1681, James Graham, 3rd Marquis of Montrose purchased Buchanan House and lands. Although the Place of Buchanan was located in a borderland between Highland and Lowland – in times of clan conflicts, the sympathies of the Buchanans were Highland. The stones from the remainder of this building after a fire destroyed it in 1852 were incorporated into Buchanan Castle and Buchanan Castle Golf Club House.

From this 'Place of Buchanan' at Westermains, Drymen, the Buchanan diaspora spread out and I feel it is important to visit some of these 'homes' of this 'colonial spread'. This will help to establish the evidence that proves that they made up their minds, acted on their beliefs and survived, and ultimately his (Anselan's) descendants prospered. It was not possible to ascertain all of the movements of the younger sons of the Buchanan families, but I have found enough evidence to make some sort of assessment of their movements in terms of internal migration from one area to another, for example to Glasgow as merchants.

In *Illustration 6* the two small islands in the foreground show how the main island is divided and is now partly submerged after the water level of Loch Lomond was raised between 1946 and 1950.[22] The smaller island is a manmade fortified island or crannog dating from the Iron Age. The larger island in the background is Inchcailloch, meaning the 'island of the old woman' - where St. Kentigerna lived. She established the first Christian community in this area, and a church was built which was the first place of worship in the area. From the 13th century until the Reformation this church had been Roman Catholic. It was used by the people of Inchcailloch as a place of worship until 1670.

Crofting (farming) ended on the island in the 1790s. The burial ground continued to be used up to 1947.[23] Many ancestral Buchanans are buried there. The Buchanans were of the Roman Catholic faith until the Reformation when most of them converted to Presbyterianism.

The name Anselan, the 7th Laird of Buchanan, appears as a witness on several Lennox charters among which one is dated 1225 by Maldven, 3rd Earl of Lennox, giving to Anselan, Son of McBethe, the small island of Clarinch, in Loch Lomond. In 1274 a witness to a charter was one Alan de Buchanan, second son of Gilbert. Maurice, another son of Gilbert, succeeded his father as 9th Laird. His name appears as a witness on a charter granted by Malcolm 4th Earl of Lennox in 1290.[24]

A number of these Buchanans appear on the family scroll with some annotations next to their names. It can be stated with some degree of confidence therefore, for example, that Anselan, the 7th Laird of Buchanan actually lived and died in this location, as stated on the scroll.

NETWORKING THROUGH MARRIAGE
for consolidation of lands and economic betterment.

Again I want to define and use the words 'colony' and 'colonist' in a different sense, not in the sense of building an empire. 'Settling' might be a useful term, but it does not really express what is meant. I want to use the words as something more - like 'building social and community networks' which would describe the different context. Another description of this sort of analysis - of partial networks or 'fragments', can also illustrate some of the characteristics of larger systems. As the intention is to show the development of these micro Buchanan networks between Ireland, Scotland and America in the context of the macro migrant flows, this would also include some networking flows from kinsfolk.

The group of people of the same nationality or ethnic group, doing the same work, or living in the same circumstances, who reside together or near one another, and are called Buchanan, are what I would describe as the 'colony' of strong inter-family and multi-generational links in this investigation.

These Buchanan migrants of earlier centuries did have strong inter-family and inter-generational links which facilitated them in their development of community ties. These kinship ties facilitated networking. McCarthy points out the compelling evidence which has surfaced to prove 'the persistence of deeply embedded social ties based on ethnicity and kinship'[25] in Christchurch, New Zealand, which reflects this notion of 'links' that permeates the history of the Buchanan migrants. Therefore strong inter-family and strong multi-generational links would appear to be the foundation of the development of community ties in any, and many, flows that develop into migration settlements.

In appraising the Buchanans' kinship and social ties, it would also appear that the most deeply embedded social and family ties were those that the Buchanans made through marriage. Examples are clearly evidenced among the Buchanan settlers.[26] Delaney makes this point when he states emphatically that 'migrant networks lessened the obvious dislocation of emigration'.[27] He also demonstrates that 'migrants in the past operated in a transnational social world and that many similarities exist with contemporary population movements.'

It is also important to note that networks are not to be seen as isolated and segregated. Delaney and MacRaild mention the following networks – communication, community, ethnic, expatriate, family, ideological, informal, personal, international, kin and friends, migrant, neighbourhood, place of settlement, and social. Add to this Fitzgerald and Lambkin's list of networks, described as administrative, business and commercial, female, local, military, political, religious, scholarly and transoceanic. From these lists it is obvious that networks can be perceived as being multifaceted, with no really clear delineation. For example family, kinsfolk and friends, religious, and neighbourhood could all be included in a multifaceted network.

These Buchanans prospered through these multifaceted networks, and expedient marriages to ladies who were heiresses to landed estates became an integral part of the networks. For example, according to the family scroll, the original Anselan who migrated from Ireland in 1016 eventually married the heiress of Dennistoun, a landed estate in the area of Glasgow. The Dennistoun family were originally of Norman descent, and the Dennistoun name appears in the records of the court of King Malcolm IV of Scotland who died in 1165.

Another example of the multifaceted network, and the acquisition of land being an integral part of expedient marriages, is in 1392 when John Buchanan, the 12th Laird of Buchanan married Janet de Leny, the heiress of the Leny estate. Evidence of Buchanans living at Leny is found in this reference:

> 'West of Callander at the junction of the Rivers Teith and Leny and near the Trossachs road is the site of a Reformation church and an ancient burial ground of the Buchanans. There is a memorial to Dougal Buchanan, the Gaelic poet and scholar 1716 – 1768, who is buried there. A monument to his memory stands in the main street in Strathyre, his birthplace.' [28]

This Dougal Buchanan was a descendant of John Buchanan and Janet Buchanan de Leny. The Buchanan possessions increased through inheritance, marriage, or for services rendered to their King or one of the wealthy Dukes of Lennox or other noblemen. For example, in 1443 Sir Walter Buchanan 13th Laird of Buchanan was granted the estate of Ledlewan from the Earl of Lennox. This was later known as 'The Moss', the birthplace of George Buchanan, the famous poet of the 16th century, and tutor to James VI of Scotland.

INTERNAL MIGRATION – the spread northwards and eastwards from Drymen to Leny.

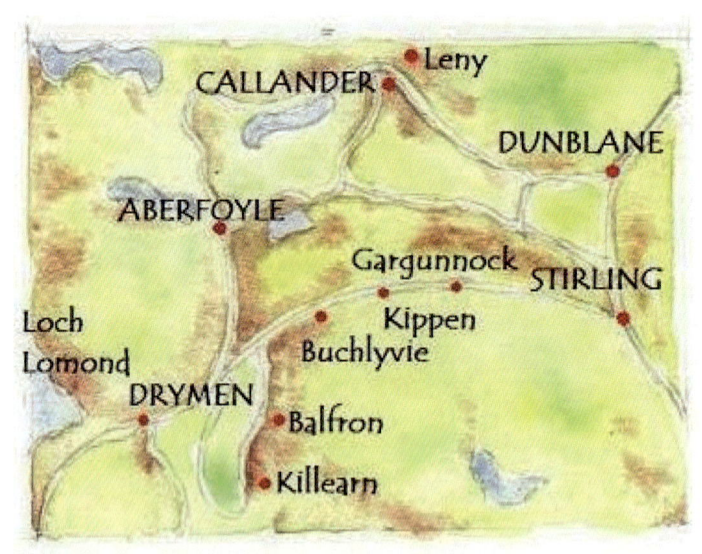

Map 6   Location of the Buchanan estate, Leny.

Map 7   Evidence of the Location of Leny Estate, Callander

'The 16th century pedigree of the lairds of Leny also constitutes the second oldest genealogy of the MacMillans. This fascinating old document, now in the National Archives of Scotland, is actually constructed in the form of a primitive tree, with *Gilespic Mor* ('The Great Bishop - i.e. Cormac bishop of Dunkeld) at its root, *Maolan de Lany* and his successors - the "Lennies of that Ilk" - forming the main trunk up to the various branches of the Buchanans of Leny at the top (the marriage of Janet de Lany to John Buchanan in 1392 eventually resulted in the Buchanans inheriting the Leny estates). There are many other boughs coming off the trunk on the way up, but few have any fruit showing'.[29]

This is evidence of John Buchanan's marriage to Janet de Leny, and the Buchanans' acquisition of land by marrying the lady who became the heiress. In 1482 Thomas Buchanan, descendant of Leny, 'Auld Thomas', acquired the lands at Carbeth.

Map 8   Evidence of the location of Carbeth House and lands acquired in 1482 by 'Auld' Thomas Buchanan who was a descendant of the son of John Buchanan who married Janet de Leny.

Illustration 8   Carbeth House, home of 'Auld' Thomas Buchanan.

In 1530 Arnprior lands were purchased by John Buchanan.[30]

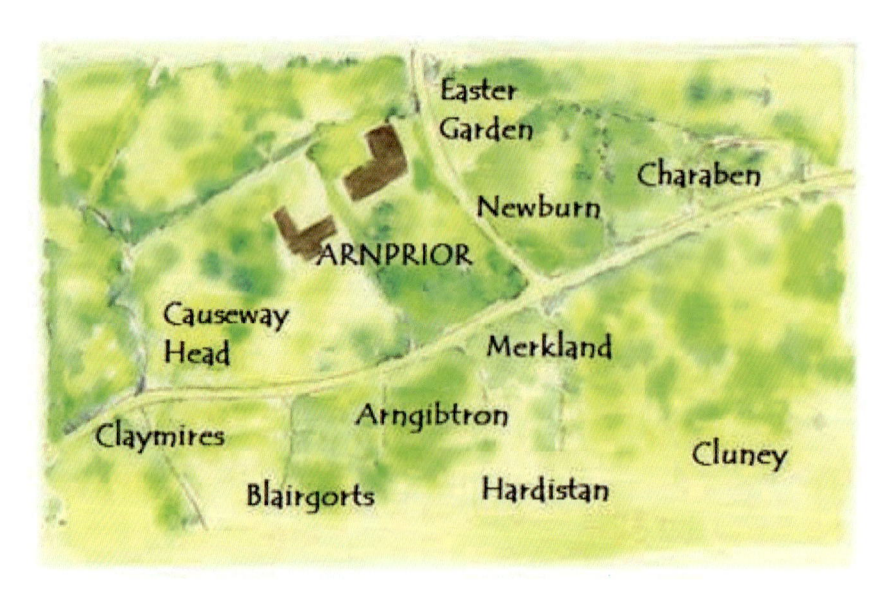

Map 9   Evidence for the location of lands at Arnprior

John Buchanan, the first Laird of Arnprior, 1530, earned himself the title of the 'King of Kippen'. The story is told that King James V and his nobles out of Stirling Castle had been hunting deer near Gartmore, in the Lennox. A royal servant passing through Arnprior was relieved of the King's venison by Buchanan. The servant informed Buchanan that it belonged to the King of Scotland, to which Buchanan replied, 'He may be the King of Scotland, but I am the King of Kippen'.[31] This story may reflect some kind of affable close relationship of John Buchanan with King James, as John Buchanan would have known that the comment would be repeated back to the King. It seems that the King was greatly amused at the incident and the two men became good friends, which meant that the King was a frequent caller on his hunting trips. In 1762 the chieftainship passed to the Buchanans of Spittal.

Map 10   Killearn - the birthplace of George Buchanan, tutor to Queen Mary and James VI of Scotland.

In 1506 George Buchanan the poet and Protestant reformer, tutor to Queen Mary and James VI, was born at The Moss, Killearn, Stirlingshire, close to Spittal.[32] I would submit that this was yet another Stewart link with the Buchanans, through education, in the network that encompassed the Buchanan diaspora and their relationship with the Stewart family. The original thatched cottage was located in the trees to the left of this more recent dwelling according to the present owners, Mr and Mrs Peter Parker.

Illustration 9   Buchanan reunion visit to The Moss, home place of George Buchanan.

Illustration 10   The Moss, Killearn, birthplace of George Buchanan.[33]

George's father was Thomas, the third son of Buchanan of Drumakill.

Illustration 11   Typical Scottish Tower House of 17ᵗʰ century.

Drumakill Castle, birthplace of George Buchanan's father, and the lands were held by a cadet branch of the Clan Buchanan, who had considerable holding in west Stirlingshire. There were many branches of the Buchanan family: The Buchanans of Auchmar, Carbeth, Arnprior, Ross, Spittal, to mention only a few, and the Buchanans of Drumakill. The Drumakill house has now gone but this is a typical representation of a Scottish Tower House of the period.

George Buchanan of The Moss moved to Paris c.1520 to study further. He escaped to France when he was to be imprisoned after crossing Cardinal Beaton. He started his literary career and returned to Scotland c.1560. Two years later he became a Classics tutor to a young Mary, Queen of Scots. He was then, however, appointed preceptor and tutor to young James VI after his mother surrendered the throne. George Buchanan is seen as being responsible for James VI's academic ability and skilled diplomacy. George Buchanan of this cadet branch was the First Moderator of the Presbyterian General Assembly from 1570-78 and the Keeper of the Privy Seal. He died in 1582.[34]

Illustration 12   Buchanan reunion visit to Cardross House in Cardross Estate.

George Buchanan's mother leased out two farms on this estate after the death of her husband in The Moss, Killearn. Another male Buchanan had inherited 'The Moss'.[35]

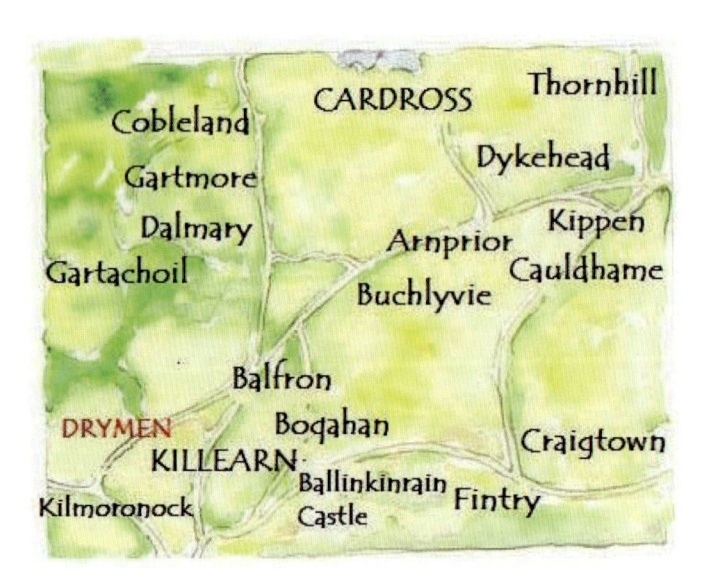

Map 11   Cardross location, north east of Killearn.

This map shows where George Buchanan's mother, Agnes Heriot, moved the family a distance of 12 miles from Killearn to Cardross after the death of her husband.

Illustration 13   Sketch of Ross Priory by P. Graham 1812.

These lands of Ross were acquired by Walter Buchanan of Drumakill, and given to his grandson by his second marriage with a Buchanan daughter of Ross of Dunblane. These Buchanans were known as the Ross Buchanans. These inter-marriages among the Buchanans consolidated the land holdings of the families of the Buchanan Clan.

By 1693 they had a substantial house erected, consisting of a high roofed building with projecting wings. Eventually the Drumakill title was incorporated in the Ross Buchanan family, and then, 'by a remarkable series of early deaths and misfortune, the male line became extinct, and the female line also continued to be plagued with all the sons dying before their fathers.' [36] All five sons died of consumption before the age of 25.

So it was that by marriage the Buchanans gained large areas of land in Strathendrick, in The Lennox. William Buchanan, 1st of Ross, purchased the Ross in 1625 from his relative, Walter Buchanan, 10th of Drumakill, and it was the family home until 1925 but the inheritance which passed through the centuries and generations was not without excitement due to the 'curse'. This 'curse' was first mentioned to me by Jean, the occupant of 'Little Blairlusk', when I called at her home to ask if she knew anything about the Buchanans who left the area in 1674 and went to Ireland.

She was able to recount many stories to me that she had heard from her grandfather, who in turn had heard them from his grandfather. These stories had been passed down through the ancestors. One of the stories is recounted here:

'After the Battle of Culloden (1746) where Bonnie Prince Charlie had his Jacobite uprising quashed, the Marquess of Tullibardine, a Murray, and elder brother of Duke of Atholl, was fleeing for his life. As a young man he had already been forfeited for his part in the rising of 1715. He arrived at the Ross and asked James Buchanan, 5th of Ross, for a safe house and was taken in to safety – he thought. But James sent word to Dumbarton Castle and King George's men arrived and dragged him away. As he left he called to Buchanan with a curse:

"*There will be Murrays on the Braes of Atholl land
   when there's ne'er a Buchanan at the Ross.*"

As fulfilment of that curse, all three sons of that marriage died before their father - the last of them breaking his neck at the "loupin' stane" at the front door – and so the daughter, Jean, inherited the Ross Estate. Jean married her cousin Archibald Buchanan 4th of Drumakill and they produced five children, Robert succeeding as 6th of Ross. However, Robert died unmarried in 1718 but left the estates to his natural daughter, Jean 7th of Ross.' [37]

Not only did relatives marry to consolidate land holdings, but neighbouring landowners arranged advantageous marriages with neighbours as will be seen in the neighbourhood networks.

NEIGHBOURHOOD NETWORKS

McCarthy points out that 'the prominence of emigrants from County Down in Canterbury (New Zealand) suggests the vital importance of kin and neighbourhood networks in directing migrants to destinations favoured by their predecessors.' [38] Examples of these networks are to be found in various Buchanan locations in The Lennox lands. More interesting perhaps is the follow-up of these neighbourhood networks displaying the same names and trends in the Ulster Plantation.

Culcreuch Castle was an early seat of the Galbraiths, once quite powerful in The Lennox. Robert Galbraith sold it in 1630 to Alexander Seton, one of the Lords of Session, and went to Ireland. This information is useful in establishing the networking of emigrants to Ulster from this particular neighbourhood location, at the time of the Plantation of Ulster from 1609 onwards, among them members of the Buchanan families, who would have known the Galbraiths of this locality. There are records of marriages between Buchanans and Galbraiths.[39] Patrick Buchanan married a Galbraith, heiress of Killearn, Bamoir and Auchinreoch. He had a son Walter (his successor) a second son Thomas, ancestor of Drumakill, and a daughter Anabella married to James Stewart of Baldorrans (one of the Stewarts who escaped being beheaded in 1425).

Edward Buchanan of Spittal succeeded his father and married Christiana Galbraith, daughter of the Laird of Culcreuch. He had two sons Robert (his successor) and George, first cadet of Spittal. Robert Buchanan of Spittal married Margaret Galbraith in 1593.

Duntreath Castle belonged to the Edmonstone family who have been connected with The Lennox estate for over 500 years. The land was granted by James I in 1434 to William Edmonstone of Culloden, and was erected into a Barony in 1452. There is a record of a marriage between Buchanan and Edmonstone in 1630 – Edward Buchanan of Spittal married Helen Edmonstone.[40] The family moved to land acquired in Ireland in the 17th century.

Again the Edmonstones, Buchanan neighbours, featured in the emigration to Ulster from this location. The Galbraiths, Buchanans and Edmonstones all had the opportunity to avail of the same information networks in a common location. Vann notes that 'Bryce, who was deposed from the ministry at Drymen in Stirlingshire for his opposition to the appointment of Spotiswood (Archbishop of Glasgow) as the permanent moderator of the Synod of Clydesdale, was recruited to Broadisland (Ballycarry) by William Edmonston, a former parishioner who had become a planter in Ireland.[41] Referring to the Plantation of The Laggan, the East Donegal Ulster Scots website states:

> 'This peaceful phase, along with the industry of the colonists, changed the appearance of the Laggan - areas of woodland were cleared, marshes drained, and roads built. The settlers also brought with them their own unique language, *Ullans,* which with some modification, can be heard in the area to the present day. Surnames from the area also have a Scottish ring: we still have Buchanans, Galbraiths, McClintocks and Hamiltons living in the Laggan.'[42]

THE SEARCH FOR BUCHANAN OF GARTINCABER

There are over 611,000 index entries to Scottish wills and testaments dating from 1513 to 1901. Each index entry lists the surname, forename, title, occupation and place of residence of the deceased person, the court in which the testament was recorded, with the date.[43] They do not include the deceased's date of death, or the value of the estate.

I selected the period from 1613 to 1800 and found John Buchanan of Gartincaber with a will dated 21/11/1755. This person's ancestors were located in our family tree. I also found an earlier match in a will of John Buchanan of Gartincaber, Parish of Inschalleoch, in Stirling Commissary Court dated 26/11/1658.[44] This person's ancestors were also located in our family tree. From this information I was able to find the farm which was the direct link to my ancestor.

Illustration 14   Scroll showing John Buchanan of Blairlusk and Gartincaber born 1545.

'The names of people and places in the vicinity of Leny in the late middle ages provide further evidence of the original Lenys' kindred connections. An inquest jury of the 1520s about the succession to nearby Gartincaber included ...'[45] Here again is the evidence for a kindred connection between the Leny and Gartincaber Buchanans.

Illustration 15   Gartincaber Farm sign.

This is a photograph of a sign indicating the location of Gartincaber farm on the road between Drymen and Balmaha on the south east side of Loch Lomond.

Map 12   Gartincaber farm 2009 and Auchmar, north-west of Drymen

Illustration 16   Gartincaber farm from a distance.

Illustration 17   Gartincaber farm dwelling house.

Illustration 18   Gartincaber farmstead.

Illustration 19   Gartincaber outhouses.
Photographs of the location of Gartincaber used by permission of the Duke of Montrose, Montrose Estates, Drymen.

John Buchanan, of Gartincaber, the first son of the second marriage of Thomas, 3rd Laird of Carbeth, and third in direct descent from Sir Walter Buchanan, 13th Laird of Buchanan (who lived about 1443) was born in 1545, according to Auchmar.[46] This concurs with what is on the family scroll. He acquired the lands of Gartincaber. He had two sons, George, his successor born in 1580, lived at Gartincaber and became 2nd Laird of Gartincaber and the 1st Laird of Blairlusk. His other son was called William.[47]

This George Buchanan married Elizabeth Leckie, daughter of Walter Leckie of Disheour, and had four sons, the eldest, John born 1629, his successor, plus George, Thomas and Andrew (who had three sons, two of whom went to Ireland, the other to Drymen). This information is also to be found on the family scroll.

John Buchanan married a cousin Jean Buchanan. He had two sons, George born in 1648, of Blairlusk, and William. George having succeeded his father in 1662 sold his estate of Blairlusk to his brother William and went to Ireland. He settled in Deroran in the County of Tyrone in 1674 and married Elizabeth Mayne in 1675.

Map 13   Location of Blairlusk Farm, south of Drymen

This is the evidence that Rae, my aunt, had requested in her letters to the various authorities - and was told that such a place did not exist in Scotland. This was my proof that Blairlusk had indeed existed all that time throughout the Buchanan generations.

Illustration 20   Blairlusk farmyard and outhouses in ruins

The original single storey dwelling can be seen at the back of this more recent building. There is a glimpse of the enclosed farmyard beyond it.

Illustration 21   Blairlusk - empty dwelling house and farmyard

BLAIRLUSK HOUSE AND LANDS. Photos taken in the 1950s.

Illustration 22   Blairlusk farm aerial view.
Courtesy of Mr Hugh and Mrs Annie Wylie

Illustration 23   Blairlusk house 1950.
Courtesy of Mr Hugh and Mrs Annie Wylie

Illustration 24   Blairlusk lane 1950.
Courtesy of Mr Hugh and Mrs Annie Wylie

Illustration 25   Blairlusk land, winter of 1950
Courtesy of Mr Hugh and Mrs Annie Wylie

It was from this farm that my ancestor, George Buchanan 'the migrant farmer', left Scotland and immigrated to Deroran, Co Tyrone, Ulster in 1674.

As Vann so succinctly puts it, this perhaps describes my mission –

> 'Through these reflections, I got to know people I never met in person, but they were real to me. I suppose their stories helped me to see the need to create the thought worlds of people whom I could never meet'.[48]

EVIDENCE OF THE BUCHANAN COLONIAL OR CLAN SPREAD 1016 – 1674

This is a map of the locations of some of the Buchanan colonial spread, internal step and chain settlement patterns of migration from Anselan 1016 – George 1674, in the area east, north and south of Loch Lomond, before George emigrated from Scotland to Ireland in 1674.

Map 14   Pattern of settlements of Buchanan descendants of Anselan from around Loch Lomond towards Callander, Stirling and Dumbarton.

CHAPTER 1   NOTES

[1] Burke, J. (1835), *A Genealogical and Heraldic History of the Commoners of Great Britain and Ireland,* 59.
[2] Duffy, S.(1997), *Atlas of Irish History,* 31
[3] O'Kane, K. (2001), *The O'Cahans of County Derry,* flyleaf.
[4] http://www.drenagh.com/history
[5] http://www.buchanansociety.com
[6] Ashdown, D.M. (1999) Pitkin Guides: *The Royal Line of Succession: The British Monarchy from Egbert AD 802 to Queen Elizabeth II*
[7] Ibid
[8] William Buchanan of Auchmar (Historical and Genealogical Essay upon the Family and Surname of Buchanan, (1723)
[9] Ibid
[10] Guthrie Smith J.(1896), *Strathendrick and its inhabitants from early times;* 90
[11] Bruce, M.B. (1995), *The Buchanans: Some Historical Notes;* 5
[12] Miller, K. (1985), *Emigrants and Exiles: Ireland and the Irish Exodus to North America,* 556
[13] Akenson, D.(1996), *The Irish Diaspora: A Primer,* 273
[14] http://homepages.rootsweb.ancestry.com/~mckinlay/lennox.html
[15] Leiper J.(ed)(2000), *A millenium Account of Drymen and District,* Drymen Local History Society
[16] Ibid
[17] Webster's(1961), *Third New International Dictionary,* 447
[18] Robinson, P.(1984), *The Plantation of Ulster: British Settlement in an Irish landscape,1600 – 1670,* 119
[19] Fitzgerald, P; Lambkin, B. (2008), *Migration in Irish History, 1607–2007,* 83
[20] Ibid
[21] http://www.clanmacmillan.org/Septs/Leny.htm
[22] http://www.snh.org.uk/publications/online/geology/loch_lomond_stirling/manmade.asp
[23] Bruce, M.B. (1995).*The Buchanans: Some Historical Notes,* 15
[24] Ibid, 5
[25] McCarthy, A. (2007),'Bands of Fellowship: the role of Personal Relationships and Social Networks among Irish Migrants in New Zealand,' 1861-1911. In Delaney,E. and MacRaild,D.(eds) *Irish Migration, Networks and Ethnic Identities Since 1750,* 191
[26] Appendix 1; Marriages
[27] Delaney,E.(2007).'Transnationalism, Networks and Emigration from Post-War Ireland' in Delaney, E. and MacRaild,D.(eds), *Irish Migration, Networks and Ethnic Identities Since 1750,* 277.
[28] Bruce, M.B. (1995), *The Buchanans: Some Historical Notes,* 14
[29] http://www.clanmacmillan.org/Septs/Leny.htm

[30] Bruce, M.B. (1995), *The Buchanans: Some Historical Notes,* 6
[31] Ibid,10
[32] http://www.aboutscotland.co.uk/central/themoss.html
[33] Ibid
Information about George Buchanan gathered from the online resources of St. Andrews University, Scotland:
[34] http://specialcollections.st-and.ac.uk/virtualexhib.htm
http://www.st-andrews.ac.uk/develop-2/musa/item.php?ID=37
http://www.standrews.ac.uk/specialcollections/Rarebooks/Namedspecialcollections/BuchananCollection/
http://specialcollections.st-and.ac.uk/Buchanancompletetext.pdf
[35] Organ, 2006;3
[36] Bruce, M.B. (1995).*The Buchanans: Some Historical Notes,* 14
[37] http://www.strath.ac.uk/rosspriory
[38] McCarthy, A.(2007), 'Bands of Fellowship: the role of Personal Relationships and Social Networks among Irish Migrants in New Zealand, 1861–1911.*In Irish Migration, Networks and Ethnic Identities Since 1750,* 179
[39] Gray-Buchanan, A.W.(1907), *George Buchanan, Glasgow Quarter Century Studies.*
[40] Ibid
[41] Vann, B.(2008), *In Search of Ulster-Scots Land,* 75
[42] www.eastdonegalulsterscots.com.
[43] Appendix II, Scottish Wills and Testaments
[44] http://www.scotlandspeople.gov.uk
[45] http://www.clanmacmillan.org/Septs/Leny.htm
[46] William Buchanan of Auchmar, *Historical and Genealogical Essay upon the Family and Surname of Buchanan, 1723*
[47] Ibid
[48] Vann, B.(2008), *In Search of Ulster-Scots Land, Acknowledgments page vii*

and removed to Ireland with his four
sons These sons settled in Ireland
as follows John and William in Tyrone
George in Munster and Thomas at
Ramelton County Donegal A ~~great~~
grandson John of this Thomas was
the grand Father of the late President
Buchanan of the U.S. Another grandson
Walter was my great great grandfather
as shown by the Chart below

    George Buchanan
    of Blairlusk Scotland

| John | William | George | Thomas Buchanan |
| of Tyrone | of Tyrone | of Munster | settled at Ramelton |

         son

    John Walter Bogue 1730
    James James " 1762
        Moses " 1804
  James Buchanan Joseph " 1846
 15 President U.S. James Edward 1869

Chapter 2   GEORGE

GEORGE 'THE IMMIGRANT FARMER'
(1648 – 1728)

This portion of the scroll of the Buchanan family tree shows George Buchanan born in 1648. He inherited the lands of Blairlusk in Stirlingshire from his father in 1662, and in 1674 he sold the lands to his brother William and migrated to County Tyrone in Ireland, according to the scroll.

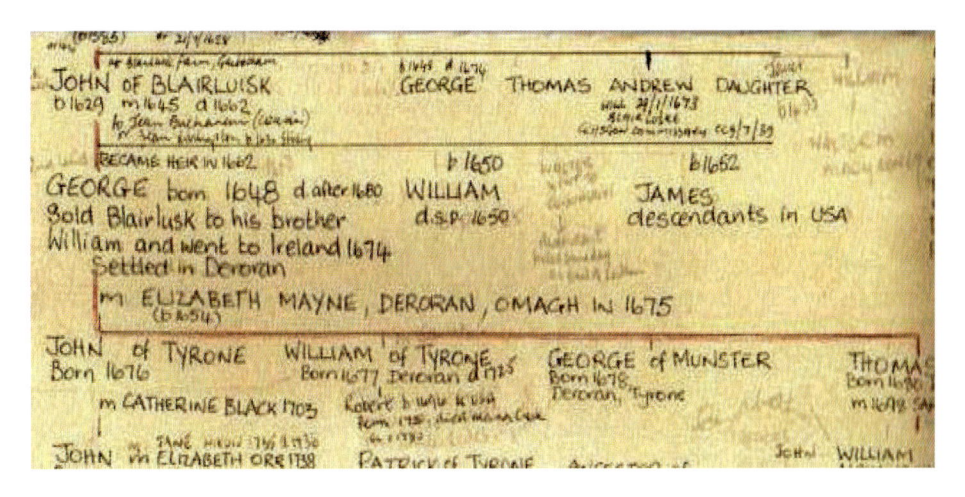

Illustration 26   Taken from a family scroll in possession of the author

    I wanted to investigate some reasons why George Buchanan had sought to leave his home in Scotland and migrate to Ireland. For example, what were his thoughts and what sort of evidence or assurance did he have that this would be a good idea, which made him willing to leave everything behind? What about his loved ones, his parents, brothers and sisters, and was he single or married? Did he ever return to Scotland? Were there any ancestral Scottish Buchanan migrants in County Tyrone? Were there any relatives in Tyrone? How did he know that he could acquire land in Termonmagurk? What were the pull factors?

On the other hand my investigation also sought to produce answers to the question of the push factors. One push factor, according to Fitzgerald, is that in the latter part of the 17th century 'the pattern of migration clearly bore a strong correlation with fluctuations in the agricultural economies of Britain and Ireland'.[1] Vann would support him in this because he writes that it 'helps to bring into focus the rural-to-rural migration pattern formed across the North Channel during this time.'[2] However Vann goes on to say that Fitzgerald 'does not explain why Ulster was chosen as a place to settle over other high-growth areas such as those found in and around Glasgow.'[3] It could be that Fitzpatrick is not persuaded that Vann's depiction of Glasgow at that time is convincing.

A vibrant, current information network within the family, or extended family, was a significant pull factor to Ireland. This is evidenced from information in neighbourhood networks about emigrant letters being the vehicle for the literate, or from the information that was acquired simply by 'word of mouth'. Business and landlord information networks and Presbyterian Covenanter Church information networks via the ministers were in operation. 'Through print and travel to the continent as well as England, Scottish ministers formed extensive social networks.'[4]

In both Scotland and Ireland in 1674, there was evidence that this was a time of poor harvests and famine.[5] This was also a time of persecution for the non-conformists. These will be discussed later in this chapter. Only by looking at the evidence will it be possible to establish what possibly influenced George's decision-making process at that time. The basic way of explaining migration is still to say that it results from the tension between 'push' and 'pull' forces, which are mainly economic; and that the attraction of another location is significant only when compared with conditions at home.

However it is debatable whether the attraction of another location has meaning only when compared with conditions at home. It depends on how the word 'meaning' and the word 'home' are defined. There are other components that may need to be taken into consideration. For something to have 'meaning', reference to a much deeper place in the human psyche is needed - for many people the 'meaning' in their life is a question ultimately to do with the purpose of living, or life itself, or living

> 'by demographic and institutional ties, as well as the political and theological contexts that played important roles in their movements and....by reconstructing the theological bases of their leaders' religious, spatial and political thought worlds, including their real and imagined communities.'[6]

Something which is intriguing, and which to some extent is addressed by Vann, is the departure from the 'concrete spatial or landscape focus' of Robinson, for example, in Irish migration studies. Cultural geographer Vann has termed it 'geotheological'- which I understand means the ways that 'Scottish Calvinism affected the sense of identity and the migration of native Scots first to Ulster...'[7]

From the text it is evident that Vann includes theology as well as geography, history, social psychology and sociology as motives behind which can be discerned the Protestant Ulster-Scots community movements. Some geographers and some theologians may not be in agreement with the use of this term. This 'geotheological' dimension is not given the same consideration, or weighting, in the equation of migration in some of the previous works on Scots-Irish migration, for example Akenson.

Not only did the 'Promised Land' pull factor operate in this 'geotheological'[8] dimension of migration, but there was the very significant push factor of religious discrimination and persecution, especially among the Covenanters, among whom were many Buchanans. This is clearly demonstrated in the information from the Covenanter Martyrs' monuments and records. Information about Buchanans has been extracted from the records and the following evidence was found.

In these records it was established that a James Buchanan was one of two hundred who were drowned at Mulehead, near Orkney, in a shipwrecked slave ship in 1679. Alexander Buchanan of Buchlyvie was a Covenanter prisoner in Canongate. He was imprisoned for attending house and field conventicles 1674 -1678, and shipped from Leith on the 12th December 1678 to the West Indies.

Andrew Buchanan, Shargarton, was a Covenanter prisoner in Canongate. He was also shipped from Leith at the same time. George Buchanan of Kippen was a Covenanter prisoner in Canongate who was shipped from Gourock to South Carolina in June 1684. Gilbert Buchanan of Glasgow, a baker, was also a Covenanter banished to the West Indies on 13 June 1678. John Buchanan, the son of John Buchanan, a cooper in Glasgow, was a Covenanter prisoner in Glasgow and was shipped from Glasgow in June 1684.[9] Other names linked to the Buchanans were William and Robert Stewart who were shot, Archibald and James Stewart who were hanged, and James Galbraith who was drowned in the shipwreck of 1679.

Illustration 27   Covenanters' Memorial, Deerness, Orkney Islands [10]

It is within the context of the push factors that an examination of the theological bases of their leaders' religious, environmental, societal and political thought worlds, including their real and imagined communities, reveals the extent to which these Covenanters were prepared to go, and die, for their Christian beliefs. This is evidenced, for example, in the Civil Wars in the reign of King Charles.

During the Civil Wars Clan Buchanan supported the Royalist cause of King Charles. However, Sir George Buchanan commanded the Stirlingshire Regiment and led the clan at the Battle of Dunbar in 1650 on the side of the Scottish Covenanters. He later led the clan at the Battle of Inverkeithing in 1651, but here he was captured. The Buchanans fought on the side of the Covenanters at the Battle of Bothwell Brig in 1679.

It is the concept of this association of a geographical location and the right to worship in freedom in a chosen place, which was a key part of the cultural identity of the Presbyterians and the Covenanters that is important. This crucial dimension of the Scottish non-conformists' *'raison d'etre'* has possibly been neglected by previous writers, except perhaps Leyburn.[11] As Vann explained in his note, 'Practical theology in Scotland at the time was set in a context that appealed to the identity of the people and their land.' [12]

Therefore when 'the land' is mentioned, the word has to be understood within the connotations of the term 'geotheological'. The lands of Blairlusk (home of George the migrant farmer) are situated in the Parish of Kilmaronock, which is one of the oldest sites of Christianity in Scotland. The earliest known record of Kilmaronock Parish is 1324. The living had been the gift of the Earls of Lennox, but King Robert the Bruce in January 1324 granted the patronage to the Abbey at Stirling. The church was universally Roman Catholic, but by the mid 16th century the followers of Martin Luther and John Calvin broke with the Roman Church and established the Protestant form of the Christian faith in Kilmaronock.[13]

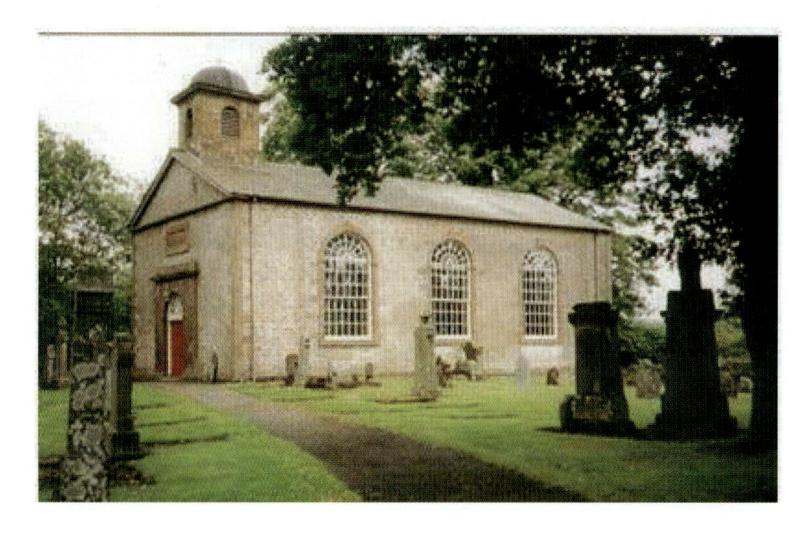

Illustration 28   Kilmaronock Church 2008

The Protestant faith was accepted here at Kilmaronock in 1548, causing a split in the church, and the Blairlusk Buchanans converted at this time to the Protestant form of the Christian faith. George Buchanan of The Moss, 'the migrant scholar' had converted, though not a Covenanter, and eventually became the first Moderator of the General Assembly of the Presbyterian Church of Scotland in 1567.

There is this link of conversion from the Roman Catholic form of the Christian faith to the Protestant form of the Christian faith between George 'the scholar' and George 'the migrant farmer', whose ancestors converted around 1548 in Kilmaronock. George 'the scholar' had fled from the burning at the stake that his five compatriots had experienced in the earlier 16th century. From the records that are available about religious persecution at the time, George 'the migrant farmer' may also have weighed up the situation and made a decision to move out, as this period was very close to the commencement of the 'Killing Times' in the 1680s and 90s.[14]

In order to establish that this farmer, George Buchanan, actually owned a farm called Blairlusk, I decided to start looking for evidence among the Scottish landowners' records. A specialist historian, Cunningham Graham, points out that land records that exist in Scotland contain 'the eternal monotony of subscribing charters'.

However I now understand that it is from these same charters, and the names of the witnesses, that evidence can be accrued. According to the records the principal landowners in the Lennox were the Earls of Menteith and the Buchanans of Leny. As noted in the previous chapter the fact that Mordac, Gilchrist and Maurice O'Boquanan lived in the 12th century is evidenced by their being witnesses to a Charter. The Earldom of Menteith was inherited by a succession of Stewarts until this line was ended by the execution in 1425 of James Stewart, 1st Duke of Albany, and his son Murdoch, Earl of Menteith. The Grahams became Earls of these lands until their line was extinguished by the death of the 8th Earl in great debt and misery in 1694.

Buchanans mentioned in Charters:[15]

Anselan MacCausland, 7th Laird of Buchanan, about 1205.
Gilbert Buchanan, 8th Laird of Buchanan, mentioned in 1231 and 1274.
Sir Maurice Buchanan, 9th Laird of Buchanan, mentioned in 1274 and 1290.
Sir Maurice Buchanan, 10th Laird of Buchanan, mentioned in 1320.
Sir Walter Buchanan, 11th Laird of Buchanan, mentioned in 1373 charter from King Robert II.
Sir Walter Buchanan, who married Isobel Stuart and was mentioned in 1398 and 1443.
Thomas Buchanan, given Carbeth Lands in 1461 by his brother, Patrick.
Thomas Buchanan who received lands from his father in 1482.
Thomas Buchanan (circa 1525), mentioned in a charter in 1555.
John Buchanan (circa 1545), mentioned in 1591.
George Buchanan (circa 1580), who acquired Blairlusk estate.
John Buchanan (circa 1622), who acquired Blairlusk estate.
George Buchanan, who acquired Blairlusk estate and sold it to his brother William. George then moved to Ireland in 1674.[16]

Also in the Scottish Records I found an interesting piece of information regarding Buchanan of Leny that reads:

17th July 1695 - An Act of Parliament was passed for Buchanan of Leny for 4 free fairs and a weekly market.[17]

The Records of the Parliaments of Scotland to 1707, K.M. Brown et al eds (St Andrews, 2007- 2009), date accessed: 17 August 2009.

William II : Manuscript > 1695, 9 May, Edinburgh,Parliament > Parliamentary Register > July 17th 1695 > Legislation

[1695/5/247] NAS.PA2/36, f. 173v.

Act in favors of Buchanan of Leny for 4 free fairs and a weekly mercat

Our sovereign lord, with advice and consent of the estates of parliament, statutes and ordains that in all time coming there be four free fairs setled and established yearly at the toun of Cults of Leny, in the parochin of Callander, stuartrie of Monteith and shirriffdom of Perth, one therof upon the twenty two day of November, another upon the tenth day October, another upon the fifteenth day of February and the other upon the fifteenth day of August yearly, with a weekly mercat on Tuesday for all commodities.

Illustration 29   The Records of the Parliaments of Scotland to 1707, K.M.Brown et al eds (St Andrews, 2007-2010), 1695/5/247

Still pursuing the evidence for ownership of Blairlusk I was amazed at the spread of the Buchanan 'colony' or clan. Considering the structure of the clan, there is this idea that it consists of a faithful body of men, all kin to the chief, perpetually loyal to him by a kind of 'potent primitive democracy into some sort of blood brotherhood'. This is usually perceived as a myth, but like all myths it is based on a great deal of truth.

When I studied the Stewart Clan I could see that James VI (James Stewart, grandson of Matthew Stewart 4th Earl of Lennox) used the clan structure as his *modus operandi*. He was the Chief in name and blood. His inner circle was composed of close Stewart relatives. This is portrayed clearly in the choice of his Scottish Undertakers in the Plantation of Ulster, where the Stewart names proliferate.

In Scotland these landowners sublet whole or parts of their 'tacks' or installed on them 'cotters' from the main body of clansmen.[18] Therefore the clan was not only a political family unit, it was also an economic unit. Beyond that there was a concentric circle who claimed kinship with the King. Further out there were those who chose to be loyal to the Chief in return for his protection. I have discovered that the land holding system reflected this to a greater extent. The King gave tacks or leases of lands to the kinsmen of the inner circle.

Despite the battle interludes among the clans, life for the most part consisted of raising cattle for sale and crops for subsistence. It was a carefully organised communal system. These were known as 'tounships' that consisted of a certain amount of arable land, pasture and moorland rough grazing. A head-dyke divided the arable, meadow and pasture from the moorland. Hay was harvested from land that was too wet for ploughing. Mr Liam McCoy who now farms at Blairlusk, the ancestral home of George 'the migrant farmer', confirmed that in the non-arable areas meadows were preserved for hay for winter fodder. However, in a wet summer or exceptionally dry summer, the hay could not be harvested, either because it was sodden wet and moulded, or burnt with the sun because of the thin layer of soil. This led to starvation of animals due to no winter fodder having been stored.[19]

In 1674 'a series of bad harvests caused by early frosts and wet summers brought famine to Scotland.'[20] It is of great significance that this is the year George Buchanan migrated to Deroran, County Tyrone, Ulster. So in summary the two push factors were religious persecution of the Covenanters and bad harvests leading to a famine in 1674.

THE PLANTATION OF ULSTER IN RELATION TO MY ANCESTORS

So far I had managed to find and locate Anselan, the progenitor of this diaspora, who migrated to Scotland. Secondly, I had discovered George Buchanan 'the scholar' the returned itinerant migrant from Europe, who obviously had a considerable input into the conversion of the Buchanans to the Protestant Presbyterian form of the Christian faith, and who had become the First Moderator of the Presbyterian Church in Scotland. I had established that he was tutor to King James VI of Scotland and I of England. Thirdly I had tracked down George 'the migrant farmer' who had sold Blairlusk to his brother William and migrated to Ireland.

To answer the question as to the source of George Buchanan's knowledge that there was land available in Ulster in 1674, it is acknowledged that communication and information networks were probably responsible. This knowledge would have had to come from earlier migrants probably from the time of the Plantation of Ulster 1609 - 1625.

Robinson states that '... Scottish merchants were rejected as Undertakers in favour of lairds with experience in handling landed estates...'[21] I had presumed, rightly or wrongly, that I would find George among these Scottish lairds' land holdings in Ulster. The search for the communication and information networks that were sources of George Buchanan's knowledge of the availability of land now began.

The first search was in the Muster Rolls of 1630 in County Donegal, among the tenants of the Duke of Lennox, an Undertaker of 4,000 acres.

The Muster Rolls of 1630 for Portlough Precinct give the following names: [22]

Robert Buchanan
Alexander Buchanan
John Buchanan
Patrick Buchanan

The second search was in the Church Records of the time. Although these Scots were Presbyterians and Covenanters, I realised that their Church Records would be found in the Church of Ireland repositories. A search was made from 1668-1803 in the Public Record Office in Belfast.[23] This was successful and will be discussed in Thomas Buchanan's migration in the next chapter. The third search was in the Flax Spinning Lists of 1796 for Buchanans in the Donegal area.[24] This was successful.

More searches were made in the Civil Survey of 1655, Griffiths Valuation of land 1847-1864, Poll books 1600 - 1800, the Religious Census Return of 1766, the Return of Owners of Land of One Acre and Upwards in Ireland in 1876, the Tithe Applotment Books 1823 -1837 and the Freeholders' Registers 1727–1793. Some information was unearthed and Robert Buchanan was found in both the Muster Rolls 1630 for Portlough Precinct in County Donegal, and in the Civil Survey 1655:

'Blen mc Quin & Cullachybeg Mr.Robt.Buchanan gent holdeth ye pmisses by ye like deed of Indenture for ye space of sixty yeares comencing 14th July 1634.'

This meant that Robert had immigrated before 1630.[25] No connection could be made between Robert of Portlough in County Donegal and George Buchanan of Deroran, County Tyrone.

Other searches were made in the Precinct of Mountjoy where Esmé Stewart had been granted 3,500 acres. As George Buchanan immigrated to Tyrone I believed that he must therefore have had a network of antecedents there, if not in Donegal. The search proved negative. A search was then made of the Precinct of Omagh. This search also proved negative. The final search was in the precinct of Strabane.

I decided to change my approach and search around the area where I remembered that my aunt had told me George Buchanan had 'landed'. The place was called Bready, along the Foyle River. A search was made of the Manor of Dunnalong in the Parish of Donaghedy near Strabane on the east of the River Foyle. A search of the Donegal precinct was also made on the west of the River Foyle. [26]

I reasoned that George would have landed somewhere near to where his contacts lived. Bready was in the Parish of Donaghedy. In this search I found what I was looking for. In the old graveyard at Grange I confirmed the presence of Buchanans, and I visited the 'old' landing site at Bready, on the banks of the River Foyle where vestiges of former busy days were evident.

In the vicinity I found a James Buchanan in the townland of Altishane, Cloughesh, Donaghedy, County Tyrone, which was owned by Lowry. [27] Could this have been George Buchanan's contact? I visited the site of the old Bready graveyard and found the graves of Elizabeth Buchanan born 1848, and James Lowry, died 1753. This was evidence of a Buchanan family having lived in the area, also a Lowry family who were landowners.

Illustration 30   Grange graveyard
Courtesy of Richard Farquhar

Illustration 31   James Lowry's gravestone
Courtesy of Richard Farquhar

Illustration 32   Elizabeth Buchanan's gravestone
Courtesy of Richard Farquhar

James Lowry, born 1711, was the great-grandson of James Lowry of Ballimagorry, Co Tyrone, whom Roulston makes reference to as Lowry Corry, Earl of Belmore. Belmore owned 14,359 acres of land, and was one of the then largest landowners in Tyrone in 1876.[28] People were attracted by favourable circumstances in Ireland, or by crisis, economic, religious or political, in their home in England or Scotland. The Lowrys and Buchanans from Scotland were Presbyterians and Covenanters. Cullen describes what was happening after the initial Plantation of Ulster in 1610.

He states that:

'Presbyterians replaced Anglicans as the dominant force in Derry, in the rich lands of east Donegal and Tyrone drained by the Foyle, penetrating in force as far as the Clogher Valley, and in the emerging linen regions of east Tyrone'. [29]

I believed therefore that I would find George Buchanan's antecedents in either Donegal or Tyrone, between Ramelton and Clogher.

⬛ Baronies allocated to Scottish Undertakers
⬛ Baronies allocated to English Undertakers

Map 15   From the official allocation of plantation lands in Ulster, c1610. [30]

In the years after the Cromwellian settlements post-1650, there was a noticeable development in the nature of the immigration to Ireland. Cullen puts it succinctly:

'After the 1650s a decided and by no means wholesale change in the character of immigration becomes evident. Sponsored movement was giving way to independent immigration, and pastoral farming was more important than previously. Settlement was less concentrated because it was less subject to the centripetal forces of sponsorship.' [31]

GEORGE BUCHANAN'S MIGRATION TO IRELAND 1674

Illustration 33   Londonderry around 1680 [32]
Courtesy of Gill and Macmillan.

    The town of Derry was granted to the city of London in 1613, as part of the Jacobean Plantations. Derry was renamed Londonderry. This drawing was made approximately 70 years later and shows Londonderry around 1680.[33] George sailed down the Foyle River to the Bready landing place.

LOCATION OF BREADY LANDING SITE ON THE FOYLE 1674

Illustration 34   Courtesy of Bready Ancestry resources.

THE JOURNEY

Before I established where George went after he landed at Bready, I wanted to examine the journey and voyage from Scotland to Ireland. Illustration 34 shows the River Foyle and the location of Bready. This is the only place where he could possibly have landed at Bready. There were landing places at the Dunnalong Ferry crossing and one landing place at the Cloughbuoy Ferry Crossing, marked 'New Ferry' on the Map. I would presume it was at the Dunnalong landing place that he arrived. Having visited the site I realise that the sailing boat would not have been very large. The impression I gained on the visit was that sailing down the River Foyle with the greenery and forested areas on either side would have been most impressive in the late 17th century.

'A good quay was built this year' (1622) and *'a ferry with sufficient boates for men and horses'*

are quotes mentioned by Roulston.[34]

In the reference it was stated that the communication link of the ancient river-crossing between Dunnalong and Carrigans in Donegal continued to be an important communication link, and that this was obvious throughout the course of the Plantation, and subsequent periods.

George Buchanan had sailed to Derry from Dumbarton, having made his way to the south west, from the south-east shores of Loch Lomond, through the Vale of Leven, as was the custom in those days according to the locals.

THE FERRY LANDING PLACES ON THE FOYLE AT BREADY

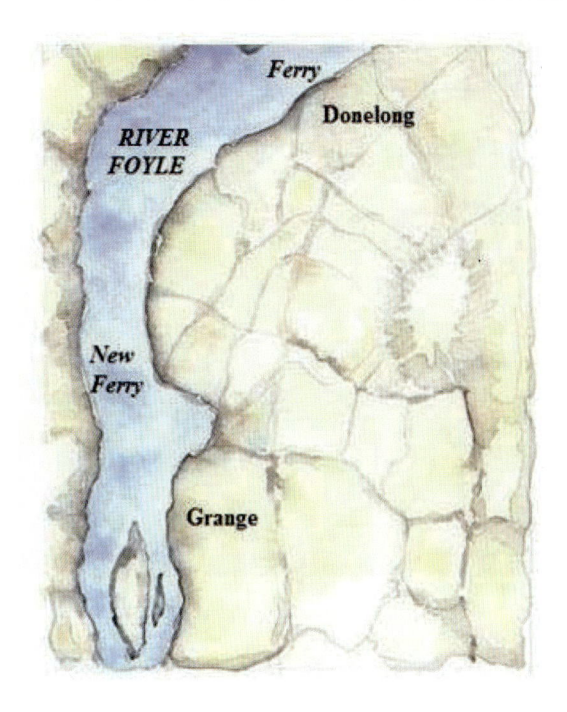

Map 16   The landing places on the Foyle at Bready [35]
Courtesy of Bready online resources.

Illustration 35   Bready Landing Place on the east bank of the Foyle River.   Courtesy of William Roulston.

Illustration 36   Foyle River at Bready Landing Place, looking towards Strabane. Courtesy of Richard Farquhar.

WAS THERE ANY FURTHER EVIDENCE TO CONSIDER IN BREADY?

In the local searches I found the following Buchanans in the search for wills.

David Buchanan, Convoy, Co. Donegal 1699
Samuel Buchanan, Ruskie, Co. Donegal, 1714
Patrick Buchanan, Dondee, Co. Donegal 1720
Thomas Buchanan, Stranorlar, Co. Donegal 1720
Colin Buchanan, Ballyloughlin, Co. Donegal 1743

All of these Buchanan names were located to the west of Londonderry in the area of the Laggan and I was, as yet, still unable to find a link with Deroran in Co. Tyrone. However in my search of the area south of Londonderry, on the east of the River Foyle and further south than Bready, I found Mary Buchanan. She was the daughter of James Buchanan and she had married John Lowry, son of James Lowry who had settled at Ballymagorry before 1641. James Lowry died in 1665.
In Sir William Petty's Map 1685 Ballimagory (Ballymagorry) and Archen (Altishane) are clearly marked, although the names of the townlands are in the old version of the spelling. John Lowry and Mary Lowry
(neé Buchanan) subsequently migrated to Aghenis in Co. Tyrone. John Lowry died in 1689.

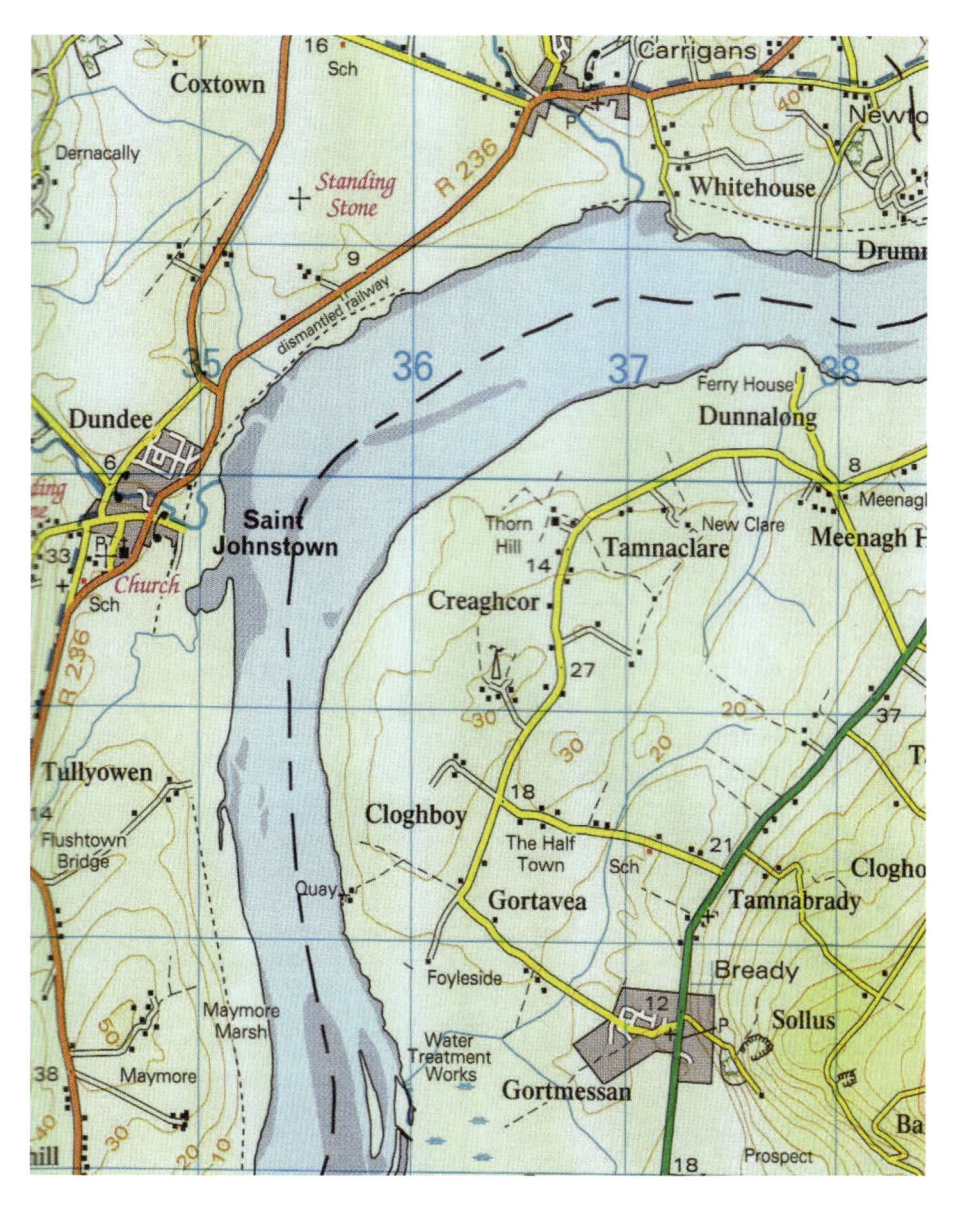

Map 17 Dunnalong, Bready – the location of the 1674 landing place. Reproduced by permission of the controller of HMSO from the 2008 Land and Property Services / OSNI Map.

The ancient grave for James Lowry, who died in 1753, in the Grange graveyard belonged to the family of the James Lowry who died in 1665. Land belonging to Lowry descendants in Cullion, near Bready, is mapped in Griffiths.[36] Noteworthy is the Covenanters' Meeting house on the land belonging to Lowry. Buchanans were in Altishane, Donaghedy (Archen, Donaghkiddie on the map) on land near or belonging to Lowry.

55

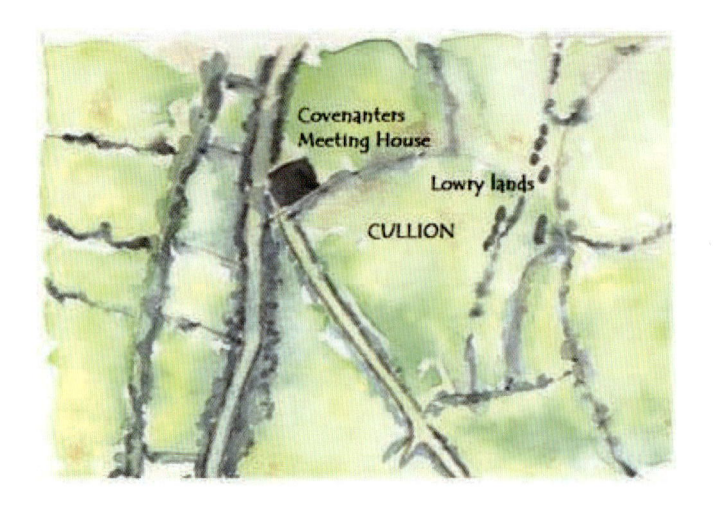

Map 18   Map of Lowry land showing Covenanters' Meeting House [37]

It was important that a connection could be made between these Buchanans of Ballymagorry and George Buchanan, who had immigrated from Blairlusk, if the 'network theory' was to be substantiated. The record for the marriage of Mary Buchanan and John Lowry would suffice as proof of their existence. In my search I discovered that these Lowrys were the ancestors of the Earl of Belmore of County Fermanagh.

The fact that there was a meeting house for Covenanters located at Lowry's lands also supports the idea that George Buchanan may have contacted earlier migrant ancestors here in 1674. There were also the Covenanter networks - especially of networking ministers who were faithful visitors to the homes of every member of their congregations, and could carry information with them.

Illustration 37   Altishane Townland 2006
Courtesy of Kenneth Allen http://www.geograph.ie/photo/197648

In 1705 Robert, the younger of their two sons, began to put together an inheritance for his grandson, Armar Lowry Corry. Robert bought the Manor of Finagh in Co. Tyrone from Lord and Lady Dungannon. Following the lead from Mary Buchanan, I discovered that Deroran was one of the townlands in the Manor of Finagh. Her grandson, James Lowry, had acquired it and it was from this lead that I was able to trace back to the landowner for Deroran, to the year 1674.

Mary Buchanan's father, James Buchanan, farmed in the Parish of Donaghedy. In the Appendix of Townlands and Proprietors I found that the Proprietor of Altishane in the Parish of Donaghedy was Lord Belmore, in 1821. He was a descendant of James Lowry of Ballymagorry. Therefore there would appear to be a connection between Ballymagorry in the Parish of Donaghedy and Deroran in the Parish of Termonmagurk in the fact that the Earl of Belmore owned both tracks of land there, and Buchanans lived in both these townlands. A search was then made for Deroran townland and its occupants.

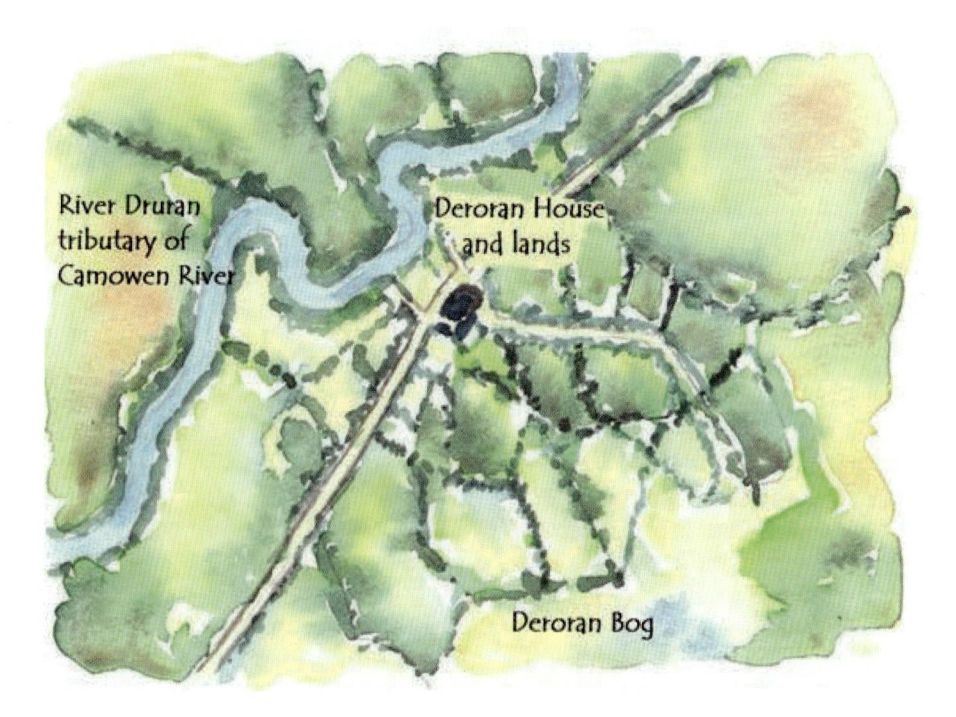

Map 19   Deroran, Parish of Termonmagurk. [38]

The Down Survey c 1655-56 of Tyrone refers to the River Druran which is the Camowen River's name in the Deroran area. Deroran is the Anglicised form of the Irish name. Earlier forms reflecting the Irish pronunciation were Derryowran and Derryewran as in the 17th century documents. The first Anglicised version that I found was in granting the Finagh proportion to Lord Audley.

As part of the Finagh Estate,[39] Deroran went through the same process of transfer of ownership as many other estates during the 17th century. It began with Lord Audley and ended with Robert Lowry, ancestor of the Earls of Belmore. Deroran is one of the smallest townlands in the Parish.

When I eventually returned to the search of the Precinct of Omagh I found Lord Audley. It stated that 3,000 acres were owned by Lady Audley (widow of George Tuchet, Lord Audley), 'neither castle nor bawn on the land; 8 lessees 3 cottagers; able to produce 11 men.' The total of the Omagh Precinct consisted of 4 freeholders, 20 lessees able to produce 41 men. Was there some connection among these people to George Buchanan? The Earl of Belmore's records reveal that:

> 'In 1860 the Earl of Belmore claimed ownership of the entire townland, the tenants being: John O'Neill, Jane McFarland, Michael Daly, Bernard McCrystal, Ann McFarland, William Buchanan and Eliza Harvey.'[40]

In this search I had found my Buchanan of Deroran.

Almost half of the townland, 227 acres of the 497 acres was held by the Buchanan family in 1860. It should be noted that in 1860 land was measured in Irish acres and in the meantime farm boundaries have changed many times. The search had been positive. William Buchanan held 227 acres of the townland of Deroran in 1860. His ancestor, William Buchanan, was born in 1705 and died 1769.[41]

Was William a grandson of George the immigrant migrant? The Buchanan name remained in Deroran for many years and Buchanans owned their original family home until near the end of the 20th century. Jim Armstrong (son of Mrs Freda Armstrong neé McKelvey) now occupies the Buchanan ancestral home. There were no Buchanans in Deroran in the 1661 Poll Tax. There were no Buchanans in Deroran in the 1666 Hearth Tax.[42] The Buchanans had arrived after 1666.

It was from this William Buchanan of Deroran that I sought to establish the link with George 'the migrant farmer' from the year of his immigration in 1674. No Buchanans had inhabited Deroran before that date. The search of the burial records followed.

BUCHANAN BURIALS IN TERMONMAGUIRK PARISH

The nearest burial ground for the townland of Deroran was Donaghanie Graveyard which was interdenominational and located in Termonmagurk Parish. There is evidence of an ancient church building there from pre-Reformation times. The earliest stone is dated 1688.[43]

The list of Buchanans of Deroran buried there are:

Andrew Buchanan of Deroran, born 1744 died 17 September 1811 aged 67 years.
John Buchanan, late of Bonnynubber, born 1785 eldest son of the above Andrew died 17 July 1856 aged 71 years.
James Buchanan, son of Andrew, Deroran, born 1786 died 25 November 1854 aged 68 years.

Andrew Buchanan was born at Deroran in 1744 and his ancestor George Buchanan was born in Blairlusk, Scotland in 1648. If George had lived until Andrew's birth he would have been 96 years old, and he would have been great-grandfather to Andrew.

The Lowry Corry Family

James Lowry (or Laurie), native of Scotland, settled at Ballimagorry, Co. Tyrone before 1641 (d. 1665)

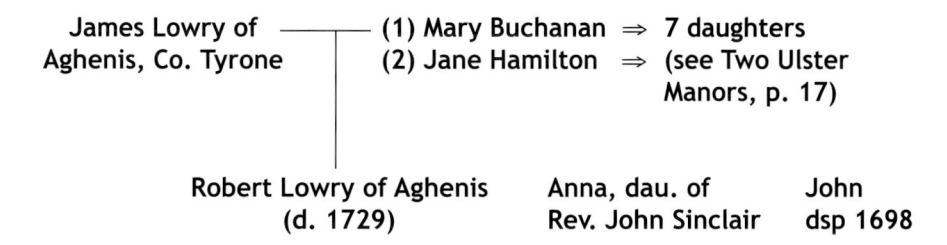

James Lowry of Aghenis, Co. Tyrone
(1) Mary Buchanan ⇒ 7 daughters
(2) Jane Hamilton ⇒ (see Two Ulster Manors, p. 17)

Robert Lowry of Aghenis (d. 1729)   Anna, dau. of Rev. John Sinclair   John dsp 1698

Illustration 38   Courtesy of Peter Marson in 'Belmore, The Lowry Corrys of Castle Coole 1646 - 1913', p 262

In trying to acquire some information about Deroran, there was not a Memoir for Termonmagurk Parish that I could find, but in the Ordnance Survey Memoirs of Ireland there is a description of the kind of farms and land around the area where Mary Buchanan lived in Donaghedy Parish,[44] and also of Clogherny Parish. Termonmagurk Parish and Clogherney Parish may be one and the same. In the appendix of Townlands and Proprietors, the townland of Altishane is owned by Lord Belmore.[45] A description of the area notes that the farms in Donaghedy Parish were in general about 20 acres and very few of them were enclosed. The details are:

> 'Potatoes are the general preparation crop throughout this parish. The usual rotation as follows according to the soil; potatoes, barley, flax, oats; potatoes, oats, flax; oats, potatoes, oats. Flax is never sown after potatoes except near the mountains. Draining and enclosing the land would very much contribute to the improvement of the soil throughout this parish. There is very little pasture here unless near the mountains.'[46]

The rents in 1829 were as follows:

> 'The best arable land is let at one pound 14 shillings per acre, the middling at one pound two shillings and nine pence, the worst at twelve shillings. Ditto in the mountains. The best is let at one pound, middling at twelve shillings and the worst at six shillings per acre. The food for farmers was potatoes, milk and butter with seldom any animal food. The inhabitants are hardy and healthy. The prevalent diseases are pleurisy, rheumatism and weakness in the limbs.'[47] 'The farms in Clogherny Parish in appearance are generally good. It possesses fine valleys and large sweeps of accessible ground drained by small rivers. The land is not usually so well cultivated as the adjacent parishes but the soil is good and, if properly managed, might be rendered as productive as the parish of Drumragh. The landscape is enlivened by gentlemen's seats, plantations and groups of trees, and the parish considered as a whole is equal if not superior to most of those adjacent. It is drained by a small stream dividing it from Termonmaguirk, which at the parish of Cappagh falls into the Camowen. The principal proprietors are Lord Belmore, Colonel Verner, Mr James Lowry, Mrs Perry, Messrs James and John Galbraith.'[48]

These descriptions of farming life in the late 17th, 18th and 19th centuries did not vary to any great extent. Therefore this maybe gives some indication of the kind of farming taking place in Deroran at that time, located in the area known as Termonmagurk and Clogherny Parish.

Therefore, whether or not after George Buchanan landed at Bready and subsequently made contact with this James Buchanan of Altishane, is not really an issue. What is important is the actual link through the Lowrys and the Manor of Finagh which is where George Buchanan settled in the farm at Deroran, and the marriage of Mary Buchanan to John Lowry, son of James Lowry (of the Earls of Belmore), owner of the lands at Deroran. I found other information available in various sources about Buchanans of Deroran.

Townland of Deroran, Parish of Termonmagurk, Co. Tyrone.

DATE	SOURCE	REFERENCE	NAME
19 May 1829	The Strabane Morning Post MBL	Freeholders' Register for Co Tyrone	James Buchanan
01 Jan 1700	CMS Data Base, UAFP, Omagh	FEP 01/01/1700 Doc No 9001055	George Buchanan
April 1857	Griffiths Valuation of Land	PRONI online resources, Belfast	William Buchanan
15 Nov 1844	The Tyrone Constitution MBL	Highest Cess-Payers 1844	James Buchanan
4 Oct 1879	PRONI, Belfast	Will - Full Abstract	Robert Buchanan
Born 1705	PRONI, Belfast	Died 1769	William Buchanan
25 Feb 1893	PRONI, Belfast	Will - Full Abstract	Andrew Buchanan

Deroran

George Buchanan b. 1648 m. Elizabeth Mayne

John Buchanan b. 1676 m. Catherine Black

John Buchanan b. 1704 m (1) Jane Nixon 1736
m (2) Elizabeth Orr 1738

William Buchanan b. 1705
Inherited Deroran

Dr John Buchanan b. 1736
only issue of Jane Nixon

Andrew Buchanan b. 1744

John Buchanan b. 1785
Inherited Bonnynubber

James Buchanan b. 1786
Inherited Deroran

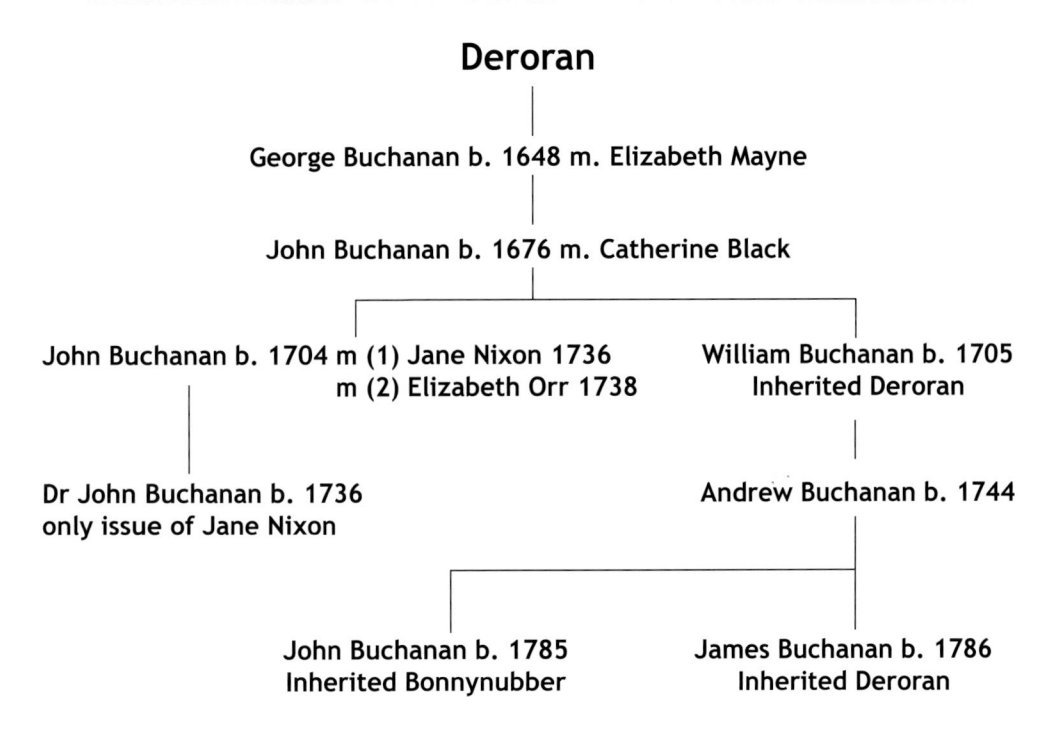

Illustration 39   Buchanan of Deroran Ancestry

Illustration 40   Farmland at Deroran

Illustration 41   Front avenue to Deroran House showing the plaque stating that Deroran is the ancestral home of President Buchanan.

Another form of evidence I discovered is that which the Genealogist for the Buchanan Clan Society International has stated in a Clan Society publication:

> *'John Buchanan was born at Deroran in 1676'.*

This would be John Buchanan, the eldest son of the immigrant George Buchanan who arrived in 1674 and is named on my family scroll.

There is also a statement that:

> *'a will for Elizabeth Buchanan (neé Mayne) is recorded 15 May 1681, this would indicate that Elizabeth Mayne died shortly after Thomas' birth.'*

These two statements lead me to believe that:

John was the son of George, born at Deroran, two years after the date of George's immigration in 1674. Elizabeth Mayne was the wife of George Buchanan (also stated on our family scroll). Elizabeth died in 1681 shortly after the birth of their youngest child, Thomas, in 1680.

Thus, having approached the search for proof of George Buchanan's acquisition of Deroran in 1674 from many different angles, it can be shown from the evidence available that there is sufficient proof that this was the case. This authenticates what is written on the family scroll, namely that of the fact that George Buchanan really did migrate from Blairlusk, near Loch Lomond, Scotland to Ulster in 1674 and lived his life and raised a family in and around Deroran.

With regard to the networking among the non-conformist Presbyterians and Covenanters, the family story includes the report that 'they walked to church'. The fact that there are so many Buchanans buried in the Old Donaghanie Graveyard leads me to believe that, as Covenanters, they worshipped with the Presbyterians at Clogherney Presbyterian Church close by - because there was no Covenanters Meeting House. Clogherney was one of eight congregations in Omagh Presbytery that can trace its origins back to the 17th century.

> 'The infant Presbyterian congregations often faced persecution from the Anglican aristocracy. Individual ministers often had responsibility for services in several locations, for example Rev Robert Wilson in Termonmagurk (Clogherney) and The Omry (Omagh), Longfield (Drumquin) and Pettigo.' [49]

Illustration 42   Clogherney Church, Termonmagurk.
Photo courtesy of Richard Farquhar

Clogherney Presbyterian congregation was formed about 1655 and the first minister, Rev Robert Wilson (1655-60) died later in Derry during the siege. This photograph shows the present church which was opened in 1902.[50] I was shown the original location of the first Presbyterian Meeting House, the 'wooden hut' church across the road in a hollow.

Therefore I was able to conclude that there was strong evidence for the story that George Buchanan lived in Deroran from the year 1674 and probably worshipped in Clogherney Church a few miles down the road. They had walked to church.

Mrs Freda McKelvey (neé Armstrong) whose family lived on the Buchanan farm told me, "My grandfather, Archie Adams, bought the farm about 1900. He bought it from the Buchanans. That was Mrs Buchanan and her brother. The farm was 167 acres. There were 100 acres of bogland and 67 acres of rough grazing. My mother was Olive Adams who married Robert Armstrong from Gortin. My mother told me that the land was all pasture land, but we grew turnips for winter feeding. We had sheep, cattle and milking cows. In the yard you can still see the old farmstead and the cotter house. You can also see the turnip house. The name of the River is the Cloughfin and it runs north of the townland of Deroran. As far as I know those Buchanans are buried in Edenderry graveyard".

CHAPTER 2   NOTES

[1] Fitzgerald,P. (2004), 'Black '97': Scottish migration to Ulster in the 1690s in Kelly, W. and Young, J. (eds.) Ulster *and Scotland 1600-2000: History, Language and Identity* (Four Courts Press, Dublin, 2004), 71-84.
[2] Vann, B. (2008), *In Search of Ulster-Scots Land*, 11
[3] Ibid, 11
[4] Ibid , 67
[5] Fitzgerald, P.and Lambkin, B.,(2008), *Migration in Irish History,* 1607 – 2007, 106
[6] Vann, B. (2008), *In Search of Ulster-Scots Land*, 164
[7] 'Geotheology' refers specifically to the role of space or place in the worship of God, but because most places in C17th Britain were the homes of people with a common past and a psychological bond with each other – a community – and perhaps a nation (for example, a Scottish, English or British one), place was a key part of cultural identity. Practical theology in Scotland at the time was set in a context that appealed to the identity of the people and their land; however, it is doubtful that the theologians of the time consciously knew this, for their writings suggest that they themselves felt Scotland was especially chosen by God for work in the unfolding drama of Providence'. Vann, notes, 213.
[8] Vann, B. (2008), *In Search of Ulster-Scots Land*, 213
[9] Ramsey McHaffie, M. (2004) CD ROM *Covenanter Martyrs and Transportees: an annotated index of People, Places, and Events in Scotland and America* CMS 301100/304.8
[10] http://www.ayrshirehistory.org.uk/Shorts/deerness.htm
[11] Leyburn, J. (1962), *The Scotch Irish; A Social History,* 105 - 106
[12] Vann, B. (2008), *In Search of Ulster-Scots Land*, 213
[13] *Information from a leaflet of the history of the church, published by Kilmaronock church in 2006*
[14] Appendix III, *The Killing Times*
[15] Thomson, J. (2009), *Photographic Negatives of Scottish Charters 1170-1770.* The National Archives of Scotland, Ref: NRAS2399
[16] Appendix IV, *Sasines of the Lands held by the Buchanans in the Lennox 1461-1515*
[17] Brown,K.M.et al (eds), 2009, *Records of the Parliaments of Scotland to 1707. www.rps.ac.uk* Date accessed 17/08/2010
[18] A tack is a smallholding. A cotter is a peasant tenant.
[19] Personal comment
[20] www.Scotland.org.uk/guide/seventeenthcentury.
[21] Robinson, P.(1984),*The Plantation of Ulster: British Settlement in an Irish landscape,1600 - 1670.*Dublin: Gill and Macmillan, 80.
[22] Appendix V; Muster Rolls County Donegal 1630
[23] Appendix VI; Church of Ireland Records 1668-1803

[24] Appendix VII; Flax Growers List 1796
[25] Appendix VIII; Civil Survey 1655 Parish of Raphoe
[26] Appendix IX; Searches of Donegal Precinct.
[27] Roulston,W.(2000) Landlordism and Unionism in Tyrone, 1885–1910, in *Tyrone:History and Society;* Dillon, C. and Jeffries,H.(eds), 742
[28] Ibid
[29] Cullen, L.M. (1981),*The Emergence of Modern Ireland 1600-1900*; 56
[30] PRONI T.1652;*Cal. Pat.Rolls Ire., Jas I; Cal. Pat.Rolls Ire.,Chas I*; Simington, ed.; Schedules of London Companies' lands. 1613, *Anal.Hib.*(1938), 299-311; Inq.*Cancell.Hib. Report.*,II. The names of the townlands contained in many of the individual grants have been collated and printed in Hill (1877), 259-353. In Robinson,P.(1984). *The Plantation of Ulster: British Settlement in an Irish landscape, 1600-1670.* Dublin: 84.
[31] Cullen, L (1981), The Emergence of Modern Ireland 1600-1900; 86
[32] Duffy, S. (ed), (1997;2000), Atlas of Irish History, 62
[33] Ibid, 62
[34] Roulston, W. (2000), The Ulster Plantation in the Manor of Dunnalong, 1610-70 in *Tyrone: History and Society,* Dillon, C. and Jeffries,H.(eds), 275
[35] *http://www.breadyancestry.com/index.php?id=58*
[36] The information given in the Second Griffiths Valuation is the following:
The townland address and householder's name; the name of the person from whom the property is leased; a description of the property; the acreage and the valuation.
The second valuation of Ireland (technically known as the Primary Valuation of Tenements) was completed between the years 1847 and 1864 and has become known as Griffith's Valuation partly because of the influence of its Director, Richard Griffith. This massive project was undertaken to assess the payment of various local taxes by the people of Ireland. These taxes were linked to the value of property occupied by each tax payer. The results of the valuers' work were published in a series of over 300 volumes detailing the names of all the property occupiers (not simply owners) in Ireland and the value of their house and land.
An Act was passed in 1826 that allowed for a uniform valuation of property in all Ireland in order to levy the county cess charges and grand Jury Rates. Amendments were passed to the 1826 Act, the first in 1831 excluded those houses under the annual valuation of £3, another in 1836 excluded houses under £5
Source: *www.from-ireland.net/gene/griffithsval.htm*
[37] Information from *OS Map Courtesy of PRONI*
[38] Information from *OS Map Courtesy of PRONI*
[39] Appendix X, HEARTH MONEY ROLLS 1662 : Deroran, Finagh Manor, PRONI T/307A

[40] *Beragh Parish Community Link*, 1980. Courtesy of Hugh Ward.
[41] PRONI; *Buchanan Papers* D1627/1
[42] Beragh Parish Community Link, 1980. Courtesy of Hugh Ward
[43] McGrew, W. (1998) *Tombstones of the Omey*
[44] Day. A., McWilliams, P.(eds) 1990, 91. *Ordnance Survey Memoirs of Ireland Parishes of County Tyrone Vol. 5, 1821, 1823, 1831-36*
[45] Ibid, 9
[46] Ibid, 89
[47] Ibid, 91
[48] Day. A., McWilliams, P. (eds) 1993, Vol. 20, 25-26. *Ordnance Survey Memoirs of Ireland Parishes of County Tyrone 1825, 1833-1835, 1840*
[49] Kirkpatrick, L. (2006), *Presbyterians in Ireland: An Illustrated History*, 309
[50] Ibid, 310

with the same church in Ramelton
before coming to this country; his
Father who must have been born and
lived out his entire life at or near
Ramelton was I believe a covenanter
also Walter's son James, was an elder;
James's son Moses was an elder for 50
years & upon his death his son Joseph
(my Father) was made an elder to succeed
him. is there an old Buchanan homestead
there or do you know of any evidence
to indicate their abode while resident
there? I understand from Mr Mitchell
there are two cousins members of your
congregation named Sam G Buchanan
& that a son of a late Walter Buchanan
is living at the Clooney likewise a
widow & son of a William Buchanan living
at the Cairn Ramelton who I believe are
presbyterians; do you believe any of these
to be connected with my family;

Chapter 3   THOMAS

THOMAS 'THE INTERNAL MIGRANT' FROM COUNTY TYRONE TO COUNTY DONEGAL

This portion of the family scroll shows Thomas Buchanan, born in 1680. Thomas was the youngest of four sons, and there were daughters also in this family at Deroran. The eldest son John inherited Deroran according to the family story. The second son, known as William of Tyrone, is believed to have emigrated to America and is the ancestor of Buchanans of Meadsville, Pennsylvania. The third son, known as George of Munster, is believed to have also emigrated to America and is the ancestor of the Buchanans of Louisville, Kentucky. My question is: why did Thomas, the fourth son, decide to migrate internally to Donegal and to Ramelton in particular, rather than joining his brothers in America at the turn of the century? Was this step migration?

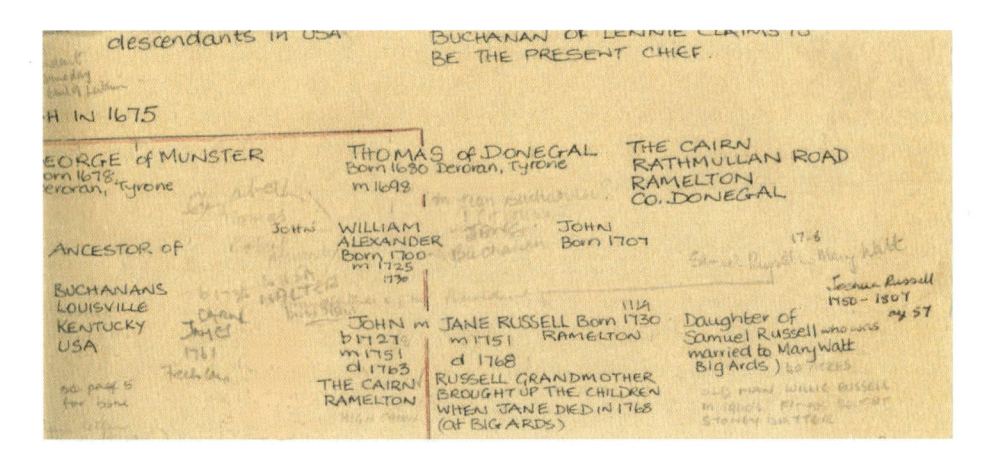

Illustration 43   Taken from a family scroll in possession of the author

What was happening in Ramelton at the turn of the century, circa 1700, when Thomas Buchanan migrated there? For some time it had been accepted that the period of 1717-1718 was the beginning of the emigration of Ulster Presbyterians to colonial America. However Fitzgerald and Lambkin point out that:

> 'the difficult years 1683–1684 saw Scots settlers in west Ulster nervous about religious persecution and payment of the next instalment of rent. They used the threat of emigration as a bargaining tool with the landlords... in the east of Donegal a number of Presbyterian ministers, such as Francis Makemie of Ramelton, who went on to become the 'father' of American Presbyterianism, made their way to the Chesapeake area in the early 1680s.' [1]

They suggest that the movement to Chesapeake, Maryland and New Jersey totalled about 1,000 around this time, and that among the emigrants were the Quakers who 'shaped trans-oceanic networks'. In the meantime William Penn had founded his colony in Pennsylvania where 'many other friends were enjoying religious liberty'.[2] Did Thomas Buchanan, through the Presbyterian Church network, hear about what was happening in Ramelton, and about preparations being made for emigration to America in the foreseeable future? Was there some familial connection with the area?

Cullen gives us another perspective to consider:

> 'The problem of a place for the sons was a crucial one in this status-conscious society, because success or failure determined the standing of the family, both in the case of cadet branches of Protestant families and in the case of Catholic families who had failed to hold on to acres in fee. The renting of land on advantageous long leases was one path to success.' [3]

Was there a long lease for offer in the Ramelton area that was available through the landlord network?
Again, as Cullen points out –

> 'The most important function of the landlord....was that of controlling settlement on the estate, whether on the individual farm or on the estate at large... in the 1650s with an under populated countryside, landowners were sometimes obliged to resume sponsored immigration, an uneven pattern of which can be traced into the 1670s or early 1680s.' [4]

Had the emigration to the Chesapeake area been part of the cause of this under populated countryside in east Donegal?

Did the landlord William Stewart sponsor or facilitate Thomas Buchanan's migration from Deroran to Ramelton? Perhaps it was not so much the help of the landlord, but other push factors towards America - like the sermons of the Presbyterian ministers according to one witness. Although there was the attraction of long leases and the opportunities to emigrate to America, Miller also points out that in 1729, for example, an Ulster magistrate commented that:

> 'Presbyterian ministers have taken shear pains to seduce their poor ignorant hearers, by bellowing from the pulpits... that God had appointed a country for them to dwell... and desires them to depart thence, where they will be freed from the bondage of Egipt and goe to ye land of Cannan'.[5]

Perhaps the Presbyterians were also being encouraged to go by the ruling powers. William King, the Anglican bishop at the time, was convinced 'that the Anglican community in the island would be swamped by Presbyterians'. Cullen also has emphasised the fact that 'it was the dramatic advance of the Presbyterians ....which accounts for the almost hysterical fears (of being swamped) in the 1690s.'[6]

The second possible reason is that some of the best agricultural land in Donegal is to be found in the neighbourhood of Ramelton. Perhaps this gives a clue why Thomas Buchanan left Deroran, in County Tyrone, and migrated there. According to *Slater's National Commercial Directory for Ireland* (1846) the produce that was shipped out of Ramelton would seem to provide the evidence that there was good quality agricultural land - 'the trade in corn is considerable....'[7]

Exports by ship of the produce from the land were recorded in the history of the growth of Ramelton which dates back to the Plantation of Ulster. Ramelton or Rathmelton (Gaelic: Ráth Mealtáin) was once a principal port in this area. In *Pynnar's Survey* of 1618 it is described as being founded in the early 17th century by Sir William Stewart, a Servitor, who built a castle of lime and stone, slated, 48 feet long, 23 feet wide and 34 feet high, with three or four round flankers on the top and a round turret 42 feet high, with a battlement and platform. Adjoining the castle was a house of lime and stone, 64 feet long, 20 feet wide and 1½ storeys high, slated, with a guard house for soldiers, and also adjoining, a bawn of lime and stone, 80 feet square, 14 feet high and 14 feet thick.

Illustration 44   Sir William Stewart's Castle ruins
Photo courtesy of Leslie Buchanan and Martin Mooney

Illustration 45   Bridge End, Ramelton
Courtesy of http://www.ramelton.net/Photos/yesterday.htm

    Near the castle was a town erected by Sir William Stewart, consisting of 45 houses and cabins, thatched, inhabited by 57 families, all British, in which there was a street, from the castle to the foundation of a church. Inhabitants were leaseholders for life (40); leaseholders for years (10); British men (23), of whom 13 were armed.[8]

The search for Thomas began. Was he in some way connected to any of the 57 families that had been established in Ramelton in the early 17th century? Was there a Buchanan amongst the immigrants there? Could he be located amongst the gradual growth of inhabitants of the area? I decided to check the Muster Rolls of 1630. I found Robert, Alexander and John Buchanan. Was Thomas connected in any way to any of these three Buchanans in the Muster Roll for the Barony of Rapho in Donegal?

Barony de Rapho

> *The Lord Duke of Lynox, undertaker of 4000 acres, his men and armes:*
> *Robert Leackye, James Wood, Andrew Wood, Mathew Lyndsey, William Douglas, Robert Lyndsay,* Robert Buchanan, *John Galbreath,* Alexander Buchanan, *Alexander Lawder, James Denniston elder, Andrew Royare, William Laughlan, John Lowrye, John Ralston, William Cokeran, Hector Hinman, Robert Cocheran,* John Buchanan.[9]

I was unable to find the exact location of these Buchanans, but the search did reveal that there were Buchanans in County Donegal from the time of the Plantation of Ulster, and maybe earlier. Therefore there was a possible link somewhere with Thomas in Deroran, County Tyrone. In order to progress the search for Thomas I decided to investigate the town and area of Ramelton and its history to see if there were any clues to follow, in the line of business or exports that would enable me to make the link. By 1837 there were 1,783 inhabitants, according to *Lewis's Topographical Dictionary (1837),* describing Ramelton as:

> 'a market and post-town, in the Parish of Aughnish, Barony of Kilmacrennan, County of Donegal and Province of Ulster... Here are extensive corn-mills, a brewery, bleach-green, and linen manufactory, and a considerable quantity of linen is made by hand in the vicinity. A market for provisions is held on Tuesday, and on Thursday and Saturday for corn; and fairs are held on the Tuesday next after May 20th, Nov. 15th, and on the Tuesday after Dec.11th... There is a small salmon fishery.'

Illustration 46   The Quays Ramelton
Courtesy of http://www.ramelton.net/Photos/yesterday.htm [10]

Illustration 47   Ramelton

Courtesy of http://www.ramelton.net/Photos/yesterday.htm [11]

     From 1714 to 1830, Ramelton grew and prospered and was at the height of its prestige. Fortunes had been made from linen, because Ramelton had Donegal's biggest linen bleaching works. In exchange for linen, corn, meat and fish, the ships from the Caribbean anchored in Lough Swilly and unloaded exotic cargoes at Ramelton.[12]

MAP LOCATION OF RAMELTON

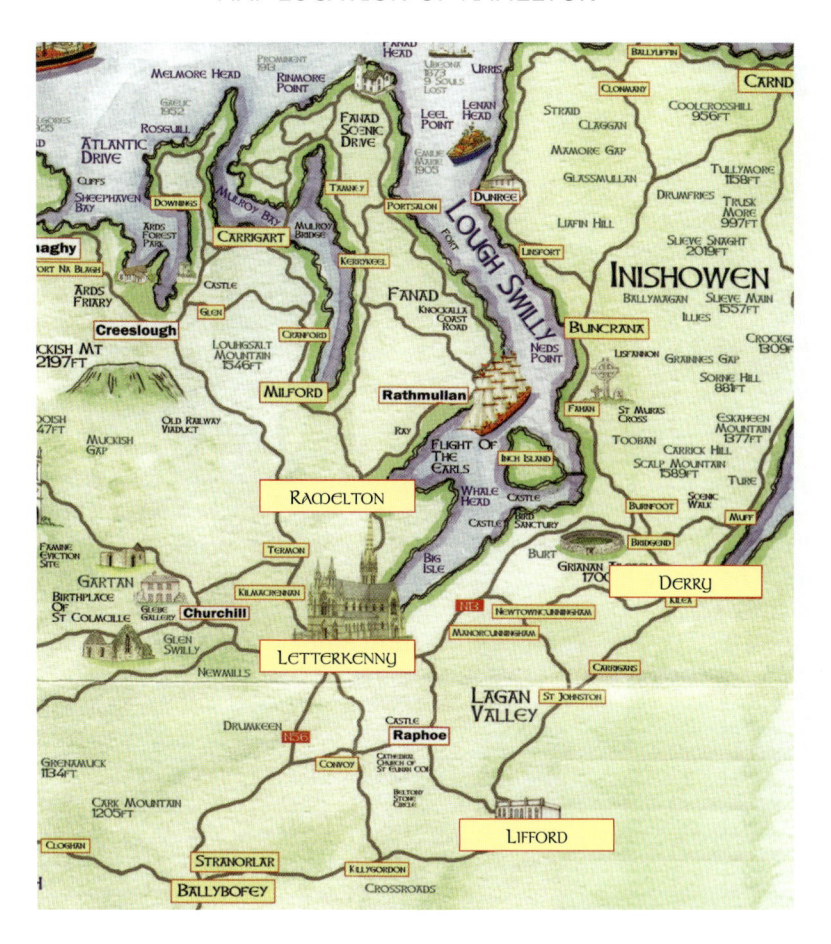

Map 20   Location of Ramelton, County Donegal [13]
Courtesy of Báid Farantóireachta Arainn Mhóir, iUlster.org and Brendan Foley

By 1841 the number had decreased to 1,428 inhabitants. The occupations included: Andrew Patton, Castle Street, corn merchant, miller and brewer; George Bond, grocer and ironmonger (dealer in iron and hardware), Bridge End; Henry White, leather seller and tanner, Bridge Street; and Mary Hunter, druggist, Bridge Street. The population of Ramelton in 2006 was 1,088.[14] The port had gone into decline.

Thomas Buchanan's migration to Ramelton in County Donegal, in or around 1700, and his great-grandson James' subsequent migration to Pennsylvania in 1783 cannot be seen as two totally distinct migrations. There was evidence that they were linked by familial networks, landlord networks, business and trade as well as Presbyterian Church networks.

It was difficult to decide where to continue the search for Thomas Buchanan, so a study was made of the changing face of Ireland at that time in order to establish the degree to which emigration was a major factor.

The latter half of the eighteenth century according to Professor J. C. Beckett 'brought some remarkable changes in the social, economic and political life of Ireland.' [15] This is true, but it is not the whole truth according to Vann, who would now argue that 'there is also the remarkable change in the spiritual or religious dimension in the lives of the migrants of this era'. He argues that 'the Stuart policies had pitted one ethnic-religious group against another', and in this he was quoting the conclusions reached by Martin Marger.[16] The ethnic-religious groups he referred to consisted of the Protestant Anglican community, the Catholic Anglo-Irish community, the Scotch-Irish community and the Catholic Irish community.

With regard to these ethnic-religious groups there were a number of issues in common affecting both Thomas Buchanan's and his grandson James Buchanan's decisions, but these issues may not necessarily be solely the outcome of the 'first cause' of Stuart policies as suggested by Vann. They may have been rooted in Plantation memories, including both the Stuart and Cromwellian memories. The people's attitudes toward these issues, as Fitzgerald and Lambkin explain, could be an outcome of the memory of violence against the Plantation settlers in 1641 which

> 'was a result of native Irish resentment at their families' land losses a generation earlier and the wish to reverse the Plantation by expelling the settlers, on the grounds, as their contemporaries expressed it, that the land was theirs and lost by their fathers.'

They also state that 'as Brian MacCuarta points out - underlying this attitude lay the belief that Protestantism was heresy, and its adherents were heretics.' [17]

The result of studying Beckett's observations on these matters at that time has enabled me to understand them as the following different aspects. Firstly, there were the landlords and their view of society, the landlord-tenant relations and the resentment by the Presbyterians and others of the payment of tithes. Secondly, there were the causes of agrarian unrest linked to the lure of emigration. Thirdly, there was the organisation of trade, the coming of the industrial development of Ireland and the growth of the Ulster towns. Fourthly, there was the administration of local government, the parliamentary elections in the counties and the popular movements in politics. Finally there was the issue of religion and society. All of the above were also linked to the increasing growth in population, a main cause of tension.

In the issue of religion and society, a few excerpts from a record made less than a month after the 1798 rebellion by a Presbyterian presbytery gives us some idea of how some Presbyterians perceived the situation as it had developed then:

> 'Iniquity abounds; all flesh have corrupted their way; wickedness is openly practised and contended for; and that not merely by the profane but by the Christian professor. Inferior magistrates conniving at, if not joining with the multitude in this gross sin instead of punishing the guilty agreeable to their own obligations and the good laws of our country. Commerce and business amongst men are materially injured by this sin and the comfort of serious Christians oft wounded. The Sabbath is made a day of jaunting, recreation, business, amusements, and too many appearing to think this is the way in which it should be spent. Common news, farms, merchandise are the subjects of converse on that holy day; men assembling together under the cloak of pretending to attend divine service, for the express purpose of discussing politics on that holy day. What glaring profanation this, not to mention the practice of feasting, drunkenness, debauchery, riot, etc.' [18]

The sin that is mentioned is presumably the sin of iniquity against God and his decrees, as manifested against the planters, and among the planters. Vann explains that

> 'the Melvillian notion of the two kingdoms was at the root of tensions over governance and religion in seventeenth century Protestant Scotland and Ireland, because it represented a depiction of society and Christendom that was in direct opposition to the monarch's vision of society and the role of religion in it.' [19]

Despite this perceived iniquity with regard to some Presbyterians' behaviour, here is an instance where networking is recorded (condemned) under the banner of 'common news, farms etc' in the context of a networking opportunity 'at divine service'. Again this is evidence that the Presbyterian network system was fully operational and all who chose to avail of it were able to do so.

This search for an answer as to how the network operated for Thomas Buchanan of Deroran was pursued. How did he know that he could acquire land at Ramelton? Who owned the land there? Was there a landlord who had links with Lowry (Belmore), the Deroran, Tyrone landlord? Or was there a visiting Presbyterian minister who was able to mention to him the opportunity of available land. Perhaps he visited the flax market and met the disseminator of this information there. There was an added note beside Thomas' name in the scroll that he had married his cousin Jean Buchanan. Were Jean's family from Ramelton, and were they descendants of a previous wave of immigrants to Ulster? Had her brothers emigrated to America and left her with the family farm?

I decided to search for Jean Buchanan in the area around Ramelton, and specifically the Cairn or Carn (the location given in the story and on the family scroll), which was located on the Ray Road to Rathmullan. I hoped that when I found Jean I would also find Thomas. I decided to check the Hearth Rolls, Poll Tax lists and Muster Rolls, for the period 1610–1750, and also Griffiths Valuation in the 19th century, in search of other Buchanan immigrants and their descendants.

Illustration 48   Ramelton farmland
Courtesy of celtic-landscapes [20]

The Hearth Rolls of 1665 had reference to a number of Buchanans in Co. Donegal who paid Hearth Tax. The names were George Buchanan of Cullachy, John Buchanan of Aird, Barony of Kilmacrennan, Clandahurka Parish, Widow Buchanan of Killidizer, James Buchanan of Garrowgart (Garrygort) in Kilmacrennan Parish, and none at Kearne (Carn) or Cluny (Clooney). In the Index to Griffith's Valuation of land (1848–1864) I found three Buchanans at Carn on the Rathmullan Road a few miles north of Ramelton. On the map the farm is designated Carn Low. Across the road there is other land designated Carn High. This division may only have been applied after 1700. The names were William Buchanan senior and William Buchanan junior. A woman's name, Elizabeth, was recorded for Carn Low also. Perhaps she was the widowed mother.

The townland of Garrygort, Milford, where James Buchanan paid Hearth Tax in 1665 is not very far from Carn townland, Ramelton. Jean Buchanan may have lived in Garrygort. This farm in Garrygort had stayed in Buchanan hands until the mid 20th century. Was this the farm that Thomas Buchanan migrated to from Deroran in Tyrone c1700?

		CARN, LOW. (*Ord. S.* 37 & 46.)						
1	a	Wm. Buchanan, sen.,	Sir Jas. Stewart, Bt.,	House, offices, & land,	89	3	0	17
	b	Wm. Buchanan, jun.,		House, offices, & land,				17
–	c	Samuel Murray,	Wm. Buchanan, jun.,	House,	—			
–	d	James Coyle,	Wm. Buchanan, sen.,	House, office, & garden,	0	0	30	0
–	e	James Adams,	Wm. Buchanan, jun.,	House and garden,	0	0	30	0
–	f	Joseph Davis,	Same,	House and garden,	0	0	30	0
–	g	Elizabeth Buchanan,	Same,	House,	—			
–	h	Unoccupied,	Same,	House,	—			
2		David M'Clean,	John Fullerton,	House, offices, and land,	7	1	19	3
3 A		John Fullerton,	Sir Jas. Stewart, Bt.,	Land,	14	0	0	12
– B				House, offices, and land,	30	2	15	15
4	a & b			Flax-mill, off., and land,	41	3	3	21

Illustration 49   Griffiths Valuation of Land 1847–1864 for Carn Low [21]
Reproduced by permission of The Commissioner of Valuation, Ireland [22]

				Total,		471	3	27
		CLOONEY. (*Ord. S* 36, 37, 45, & 46.)						
1 A	a	James Heron,	Sir James Stewart, Bt.	House, offices, & land,	18	2	3
– B		John Heron,			34	1	21
– C					11	0	37
–	A a	Archibald M'Ilwain,	James and John Heron,	House, off., & sm. garden,	—		
–	B b	Unoccupied	James Heron,	House,	—		
–	c	William Logan,	Same,	House & small garden,	—		
–	d	Eliza Martin,	Same,	House and garden,	0	0	20
–	e	Archibald Stewart,	Same,	House and garden,	0	0	20
2	a	John Ellison,	Sir James Stewart, Bt.,	House, offices, and land,	23	2	4
–	b	Robert Ellison,	John Ellison,	House,	—		
3		Alexander Davis,	Sir James Stewart, Bt.	House, offices, and land,	23	3	4
4 A	a	Richard Heron,	Same,	House, offices, & land,	29	0	25
– B					13	0	11
–	b	John M'Naught,	Richard Heron,	House,	—		
5	a	George Bond,	Sir James Stewart, Bt.,	Caretaker's house & land,	10	0	5
–	b	Alexander Starrett, jun.	Same,	House, office, & garden,	0	1	0
6		David Grier,	Same,	House, offices, and land,	31	0	14
7		Robert Grier,	Same,	House, offices, and land,	32	2	5
8	a	Alexander Grier,	Same,	House, offices, and land,	30	3	5
–	b	James Cafferty,	Alexander Grier,	House,	—		
9 A		John Spencer,	Sir James Stewart, Bt.,	Land,	13	0	18
– B					6	3	31
10 A		Walter Buchanan,	Same,	Flax-mill and land,	10	1	3
– B				House, offices, and land,	0	3	35
– C				Land,	3	0	20
11 A	a						

Illustration 50   Griffiths Valuation of Land 1847–1864 for Clooney [23]
Reproduced by permission of The Commissioner of Valuation, Ireland [24]

Working back from this information in Griffiths I was able to find the Buchanans in the Freeholder Poll Book for Co Donegal 1761–75.[25] There I found James Buchanan of Kearn (phonetic spelling of Cairn or Carn), a Freeholder. The landlord was Sir A. Stewart and this was registered in 1761. The Freeholder Poll Book established that there was a James Buchanan in the Kearn (Carn), and a John Buchanan in Cluney (Clooney) the neighbouring townland, also registered in 1761. James and John may have been brothers. John Buchanan's descendant had a flax-mill and 22 acres of land in Clooney, and in Carn, James Buchanan's descendants had 89 acres as noted in Griffiths Valuation of Land 1845 – 1864. There had not been any Buchanans in Carn or Clooney before

1700 according to the Hearth Rolls of 1665. However after this date these two Buchanans do appear in the Freeholder Poll Book in 1761. This verifies the timescale on the family scroll. Did James of Kearn (Carn) and John of Cluney (Clooney), both Freeholders, migrate from Garrygort where James Buchanan had paid Hearth Tax in 1665?

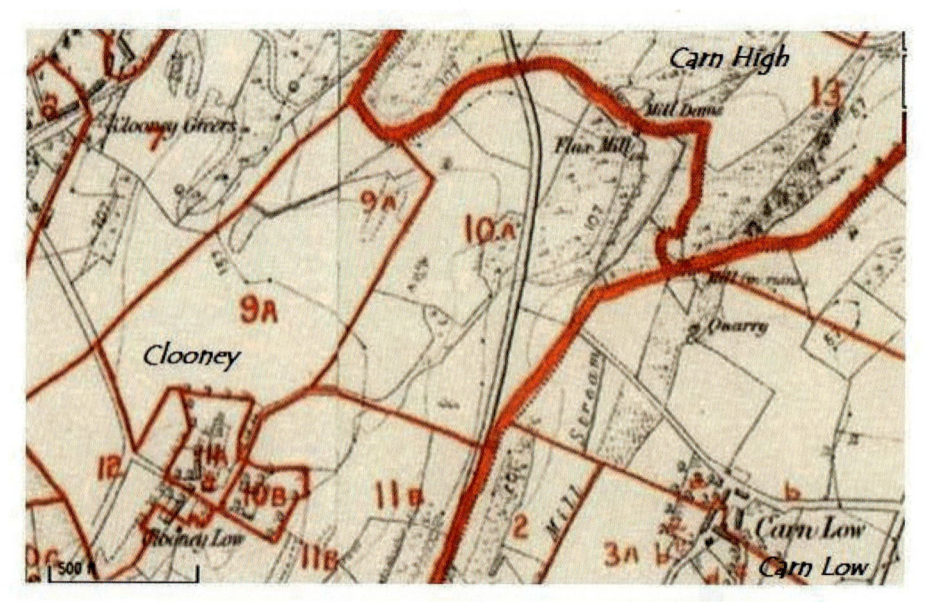

Map 21   Information from Griffiths Valuation of Land Map 1847–1864 for Clooney and Carn showing the Flax Mill
Reproduced by permission of the Commissioner of Valuation, Ireland [26]

Now that I had established that there were land holdings in Carn and Clooney townlands in the mid-1800s, I was able to work back from here to try to establish when the settlers had arrived here. For this I had been able to access the Freeholders Poll Book.

Brown, Wm.	Moneylaban	D. Chambers	1775
Buchannon, Jas.	Leatbegg	Clements	1761
Burgoyne, Rev. Thos.	Lifford	Ld. Erne	1761
Buchannon, Wm.	Lisnanees	H. Wray	1761
Jas.	Kearn	Sir A. Stewart	1761
John	Cluney	do.	1761

Illustration 51   Freeholders Poll Book for Co Donegal, 1761–1775 [27]

Another lead from the Griffith's Valuation Map was the Flax Mill. I decided to search for Buchanans in the Flax Growers List of 1796. In Tullyfern Parish I found a John Buchanan with 3 wheels and another John Buchanan with 4 wheels. I also found a Samuel Buchanan with 1 wheel and a Walter Buchanan with 1 wheel. (Interestingly where the Buchanan ancestors were located in Termonmagurk Parish in County Tyrone I found Andrew Buchanan with 1 wheel. In Donaghedy Parish in County Londonderry I found a George Buchanan with 3 wheels, and in Clogherney Parish County Tyrone a William Buchanan with 3 wheels). The Buchanans had links with the linen industry. I had to ask the question – what was the significance of the spinning wheels? [28]

Illustration 52   18th Century Spinning Wheel [29]

The significance of the spinning wheels was the fact that, before the production of cotton, linen was produced for household items such as bedsheets, furnishings and clothing, to be used at home and also exported which brought a supplementary income. Before linen production became commercialised it was a home industry. When the flax fibres were ready the women spun them into yarn. When the yarns were ready the men wove them into linen lengths which were then sold in the linen markets.

'The better off small-holders engaged in weaving, the poorer families in spinning.' [30]

> 'Home production of linen was replaced in many areas in the 18th century when the industry became commercialised and there was a massive expansion of flax cultivation during the early 19th century. The acreage of flax sown in Ireland rose from about 70,000 acres in 1810 to around 175,000 by the early 1850s. During the peak of linen production in Ireland more than 80% of it was grown in Ulster. Cultivation was highly labour intensive: the ground was usually ploughed, harrowed and rolled again after

sowing. Flax grown for fibre was usually ready to be harvested about 14 weeks after sowing. Until the 1940s all flax was pulled by hand and tied into sheaves or 'beets' using bands made from rushes.' [31]

'1761 the Trustees of the Linen Manufacture offered a premium of a spinning wheel to every person who sowed four pottles (half gallons) of flax seed. The gentry of the time gave £300 to provide large quantities of flax seed and to distribute five hundred wheels and a hundred reels of yarn to bandle[32] weavers who agreed to weave linen.[33]

When the linen was woven it was distributed through various linen markets. I found a reference to a linen market in Omagh:

'Patrick Hughes was a linen weaver, and he was supposed to have met the grandfather of the later President Buchanan at a flax market in Omagh and was advised to settle in Chambersburg, Pennsylvania, where many Ulster roots were already established.' [34]

If this story is true, then he had travelled a long way from Ramelton to the linen market at Omagh. Somehow there seemed to be a distinct Buchanan link through the flax and linen networks as well as the land networks.

'In the 18th century fortunes had been made from linen, because Ramelton had Donegal's biggest linen bleaching works. The ships that came from the Caribbean anchored in Lough Swilly and unloaded exotic cargoes at Ramelton in exchange for linen, corn, meat and fish.' [35]

Illustration 53   River Lennon at Ramelton [36]
Courtesy of Donegal Cottage Holidays

THE RAMELTON COMMUNITY

With regard to how the Presbyterians and others regulated their lives amidst the hustle and bustle of every day, among the hustle and bustle of the linen industry, and the farming of provisions of corn, meat and fish for export Vann explains it this way:

> 'the community's belief system was affected by a shift among seventeenth century Scottish ministers away from the sixteenth century notion of the covenant of grace...to a more contractual covenant of works that placed a greater emphasis on righteous behaviour.' [37]

The outworking of this meant that there was a specific 'community perception of lands and public behaviours in Scotland, Ireland and America.' [38] This may have been the result of the various waves of Scottish ministers arriving and departing Ulster who carried the more 'Calvinistic orthodoxy of the Westminster Confession of Faith 1643–1648' with them. This was known as 'the doctrines of the two kingdoms... in other words the magistrate was to support the work of the Kirk.' [39]

Again Vann carefully explains that the community that was built on these precepts in south-west Scotland expanded into Ulster...'with the polity and sovereignty doctrine attributed to this ecclesiastical community eventually being diffused to America.' [40]

The Ramelton community spawned one of these diffusers, Francis Makemie, who has become known as 'the Father of American Presbyterianism'. He worshipped in what is now called 'The Old Meeting House' in Ramelton. By 1682, Makemie had received his ordination nearby in St. Johnston. In 1683, he emigrated to Virginia and fought for civil and religious liberty. He founded the American Presbyterian Church. The Presbyterian work ethic was evident in the community of Ramelton where the covenant between God and man was reflected in the life and behaviour of the inhabitants. This was the Ramelton community Thomas Buchanan of County Tyrone was destined to join.

Today the fully restored 'Old Meeting House' is the town library. The question that arises now is - was there a link with the Presbyterian networks that Thomas availed of? Was he a young man who espoused the dreams and challenges of Francis Makemie in America? Was he planning to link up and travel to America through contacts in Ramelton? Was he a Covenanter? There seems to be a two to one possibility that he was. In Ramelton 'there are two meeting-houses for Covenanters and one for Presbyterians.' [41] There is also a mention of Covenanters meetings in America in the emigrant letter included in this book.

Illustration 54   Old Meeting House, Ramelton, side view [42]

Illustration 55   Old Meeting House, front view [43]

Thomas Buchanan remains the mystery migrant. He was an internal migrant from County Tyrone to Donegal around 1700. It is assumed that he migrated internally because the story included the idea that he had acquired land through marriage to his cousin Jean Buchanan near Ramelton, rather than emigrate to America as did his brothers William and George. Jean's brothers (Buchanans) may have decided to emigrate to Pennsylvania to acquire land also.

Similarly it was very difficult to find Thomas' sons. According to the land patents in Cumberland County, in Pennsylvania, there were six Buchanan brothers who emigrated from Ramelton at that time. The probability is that Cumberland County was the destination of the immigrants from Cairn. There were ten communicants in the Ramelton Presbyterian Church rolls from Clooney, and over the same period of time there was only one from Cairn in the mid 19th century just before the great famine. It appears that the Clooney Buchanans did not emigrate and the Cairn Buchanans did. On the other hand Thomas may have had some association with the linen industry that was flourishing at Ramelton, and had contacts in Pennsylvania for trade in flax-seed.

An interesting article was discovered in the ongoing research by the Campbell House Museum, St. Louis. This concerned a newspaper article dated 6 March 1892.

> 'Hazlett Campbell and Hugh Campbell of No 150 S Lucas Place and their cousin, Col Robert Campbell of St. Louis, who wore his 'eagles' before Vicksburg, are descendants of the Stuart Kings of Scotland. The Campbells' father, Robert Campbell, who died in St Louis, founded his fortune by "Indian Trading" like Astor of New York. He was a Scotch-Irishman from County Tyrone. His mother was a daughter of Robert Buchanan, a cadet of the House of Buchanan Lairds of Carbeth, Highlanders who were descended

from the 12th Laird of Buchanan whose wife was a daughter of the 2nd Duke of Albany, Governor Regent of Scotland, and a grandson of Robert II King of Scotland. Col. Robert Buchanan's father was a brother of Hazlett Campbell's grandmother. Captain Alexander Buchanan's great-grandfather was a brother of Thomas Buchanan of Ramelton, County Donegal, ancestor of President Buchanan who thus was also a descendant of King Robert II. Your U.S. Marshall Frank M. Buchanan is also of royal descent.' [44]

Another source states that Thomas Buchanan left Ireland and settled with his family in Charles County, Maryland in Virginia. Thomas, his wife and five sons were among the earliest settlers in this part of the American Commonwealth – Thomas purchased substantial acreage from the British Commonwealth in Charles County township.

Another online version of the story is that Thomas Buchanan of Ramelton in the County of Donegal, Ireland, was born in 1680. He and his wife had five sons. They came to America in 1730. Thomas' father was George Buchanan. The sons' names were Alexander Buchanan born 1702, William Buchanan born 1704, John Buchanan born 1708, James Buchanan born 1709 and who died in 1850, and Thomas Buchanan unknown birth date.' There are descendants of his who have recorded the fact that he and his wife and family emigrated from Ireland to America in or around 1718 -1720. The estate of Thomas Buchanan was settled in 1745 after his death in 1744 in Fawn Township, York County, Pennsylvania.

The common factors in these and earlier accounts from both Ireland and America, in accord with the family scroll, are that Thomas of Donegal was from Ireland and that he was born in 1680. There is a relationship with the Campbell family which is linked back to Thomas. He was descended from the 12th Laird of Buchanan, and was related to the 2nd Duke of Albany in Scotland. He emigrated to America. Many of these details are noted in the story from the family scroll. However the author hopes to pursue the search for Thomas and eventually be able to have some concrete evidence of his existence and his migration stories. The next chapter will include some of these findings.

CHAPTER 3   NOTES

[1] Fitzgerald, P. and Lambkin, B. (2008). *Migration in Irish history; 1607–2007*, 111.
[2] Ibid.
[3] Cullen, L.M. (1981), *The Emergence of Modern Ireland 1600–1900*, 115
[4] Ibid, 84
[5] Miller, K.A. (1985). *Emigrants and Exiles*, 159
[6] Ibid, 110
[7] *Slater's National Commercial Directory for Ireland* (1846); 527 http://www.failteromhat.com/slater/0219.pdf
[8] Hawbaker, G.(2008) *Dear William, Letters from Home 1796–1825*
[9] *Muster Rolls 1630;* www.northernirelandancestry.com/Census substitutes.htm
[10] http://www.ramelton.net/Photos/yesterday.htm
[11] http://www.ramelton.net/Photos/yesterday.htm
[12] www.ramelton.net/history
[13] *Map of the Highlands of Ireland, (2009). Courtesy of Báid Farantóireachta Arainn Mhóir and iUlster.org and Brendan Foley*
[14] www.ramelton.net/history
[15] Crawford,W.H. and Trainor,B., (1969;1978) *Aspects of Irish Social History 1750- 1800.* ix
[16] Vann, (2008). *In Search of Ulster-Scots Land; The Birth and Geotheological Imaginings of a Transatlantic People, 1603 – 1703*, 165.
[17] Fitzgerald, P. and Lambkin, B. (2008), *Migration in Irish history; 1607–2007*, 260
[18] Stewart, 1798. *Minutes of the Burgher Presbytery of Down held in Armagh, 3 July 1798, ordaining a fast as a propitiation of the '98 rebellion.*
[19] Vann, (2008). *In Search of Ulster-Scots Land; The Birth and Geotheological Imaginings of a Transatlantic People, 1603 – 1703*, 53.
[20] http://www.celtic-landscapes.de/RAMELTON/index.html
[21] Information from Griffiths Valuation of Land, Carn Low
[22] archive_mail@valoff.ie
[23] Information from *Griffiths Valuation of Ireland 1847–1864*, Clooney
[24] archive_mail@valoff.ie
[25] Information from PRONI Freeholders List Co Donegal, http://www.proni.gov.uk/freeholders/ViewBook
[26] Information from *Griffiths Valuation of Ireland 1847–1864*, Carn
[27] Information from PRONI Freeholders List Co Donegal, http://www.proni.gov.uk/freeholders/ViewBook

[28] *Irish Flax Growers, 1796*
The Irish Linen Board published a list of nearly 60,000 individuals in 1796. Spinning wheels were awarded based on the number of acres planted. People who planted one acre were awarded 4 spinning wheels and those growing 5 acres were awarded a loom. Donegal and Tyrone had the highest number of awards. These extracts contain the name, parish and county. Also known as the Spinning Wheel list or the Flax Growers Bounty. http://www.failteromhat.com/flax1796.php
[29] Information for drawing from *St Fagan's Museum*
[30] Dillon, C. and Jefferies, H.(eds), (2000) *Tyrone: History and Society,* 440
[31] *Clare Museum.* http://www.clarelibrary.ie/eolas/claremuseum/acquisitions/bed_linen_quilt.htm
[32] The primitive handloom produced coarse linen cloth of some 12-20" width known as 'bandle' linen. www.geocities.com/craigavonhs/rev/luttonlinentrade.html
[33] *Clare Museum.* http://www.clarelibrary.ie/eolas/claremuseum/
[34] Dillon, C. and Jefferies, H.(eds), (2000) *Tyrone: History and Society,* 477
[35] www.ramelton.net/history
[36] http://www.donegalcottageholidays.com/gallery/ramelton/image-1.jpg
[37] Vann, (2008). *In Search of Ulster-Scots Land; The Birth and Geotheological Imaginings of a Transatlantic People, 1603 – 1703,* 66
[38] Vann, (2008). *In Search of Ulster-Scots Land; The Birth and Geotheological Imaginings of a Transatlantic People, 1603 – 1703,* 67
[39] Ibid, 53
[40] Ibid, 54
[41] *Covenanter meeting-houses;* http://www.libraryireland.com/Lewis/LewisT/49-Tully.php/index.php
[42] *Old Meeting House* – the first permanent structure erected by the Presbyterian congregation in Ramelton with 17th century features. This was the building Francis Makemie worshipped in as a youth.
[43] *Ramelton Meeting House* - in 1811 it was extended and in 1901 it was left empty after the building of a new church, and rented as a workshop. It has become the home of the Ramelton Library.
[44] Information courtesy of Frank Collins, Ulster American Folk Park, Omagh, Co. Tyrone.

CHAPTER 4   JAMES

the date Thomas settled at Hamilton I wish to secure; likewise the name of his son & to know whether he had more than one son, also who were the sons of these sons of Thomas, who John & Walter as shown in the chart below were brothers. I believe but do not know, that the son of Thomas was named James, can that be ascertained. I am anxious to get the date of birth of Walter Buchan & name of his wife & if it can be learned the year of his removal to the United States, he must have been born about 1715 or 1720 & have removed to Pennsylvania previous to 1745 or 50, for about 1750 it was at his place that a great rally was held of covenanters in Pennsylvania, He was an elder in the covenanter church therefore I presume prominently identified

JAMES BUCHANAN

'THE IRISH EMIGRANT'

(1761–1821)

This portion of the scroll of the Buchanan family tree shows James Buchanan born in 1761. According to the story, he was the 4th son of John Buchanan and Jane Russell. There were eight children in the family and he was the second youngest. His eldest brother William inherited the farm at the Carn, Ramelton. When James was seven years old his mother died and he and his brother John aged five were brought up by their grandmother Russell (née Watt). Jane was the daughter of Samuel Russell, a Church of Ireland farmer, who had disapproved of his daughter's marriage to a 'rough-necked Presbyterian' according to the family story.

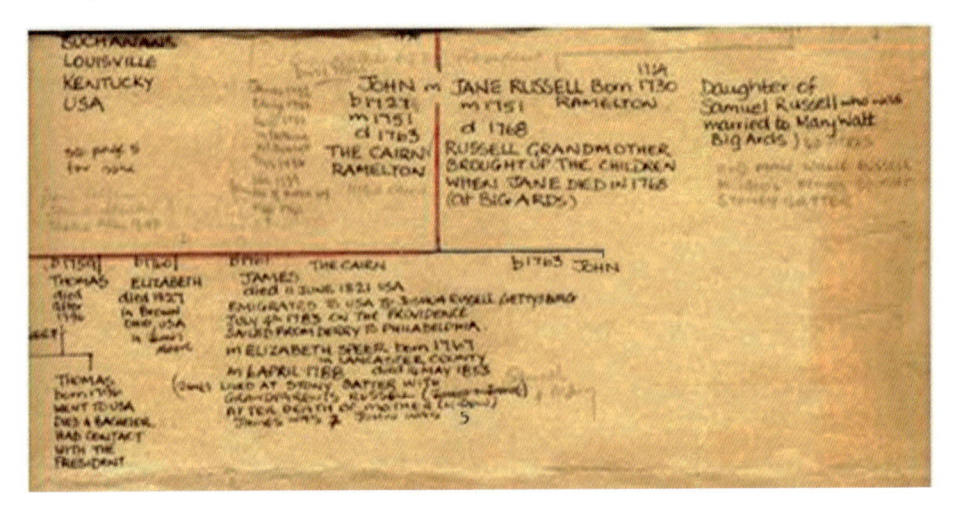

Illustration 56   Family scroll showing James Buchanan, Carn, Ramelton

The Russells lived at the farm called 'Big Ards' south of Ramelton. They had also acquired the farm called 'Stony Batter' where the orphan James Buchanan had been brought up. When James was 22 years old his uncle Joshua Russell, his mother's brother, sent for him from Gettysburg, Pennsylvania. He had heard that James was 'good at figures' and he had need of a clerk to keep the accounts at his busy Russell Tavern in Gettysburg, Pennsylvania.

The family story gives a believable account of why James might have decided to emigrate. There was already a familial network in place between Jane Russell, in Ramelton and her brother Joshua Russell in Gettysburg. Joshua and Jane were literate. Their mother, Mary Russell, could probably read and write also. James had received a letter with the promise of a job from his Uncle Joshua, and he had sent the remittance in the letter for the journey. His Uncle Joshua promised to meet him at Philadelphia. My task was now to establish if any or all of these people did actually exist. Was there any proof? How could I prove the story was true?

The questions I want to try and answer in this chapter are these: When did James Buchanan decide to emigrate to America? Why did James Buchanan want to leave his home in Ireland in the year 1783, knowing that he would probably never return there? Who facilitated his migration from Stony Batter, in the Big Ards, Ramelton, County Donegal? What were the networks in place at that time that enabled him to fulfil his ambitions and dreams across the Atlantic? Where did he go when he went to America and where did he settle? How did he make the journey to his destination and what was involved in that?

In order to answer these questions I decided to travel to Donegal first of all and try to locate 'Stony Batter' where, according to family tradition, the maternal Russell grandparents of the orphaned James Buchanan had brought him up. The problem was that I had no idea where Stony Batter might be, despite many searches. Did Stony Batter actually exist? The only clue came from a family tree in the form of a hand written rolled up piece of paper containing the information that Stony Batter was where orphans James and John Buchanan were brought up by their Russell grandparents at the Big Ards.

I made many expeditions to Ramelton and made enquiries in the local library and in Donegal Ancestry Centre. I searched Church records and generally knocked on doors in the locality. The same answer prevailed. That Buchanan line had died out, or they had gone away.

However I did not intend to give up but kept returning, asking questions of the locals and keeping in touch with the area. Then in 2006 I had my big break. Once more I drove along the narrow country roads and to my astonishment found the following item displayed at the Carn. It was positioned beside a very pretty Irish cottage that was obviously now being lived in. There had been no occupants there previously.

Illustration 57   Notice at Carn High, Ramelton.

It reads: 'I, Mark Buchanan, intend to apply for permission for development at this site at Carn High, Ramelton, County Donegal. The development will consist of the erection of a dwelling house and domestic garage with septic tank. The planning application may be inspected at the offices of the planning authority at Civic Offices, Main Street, Milford, County Donegal. A submission or observation in relation to the application may be made in writing to the planning authority on payment of a fee of 20 Euro.'

Illustration 58   Carn High Buchanan home

Illustration 59   Sarah Ferguson neé Buchanan who lives in the cottage.

    I was able to make contact with these Buchanans and had many conversations with Sarah Buchanan who is now 96 years old. It transpired that they were returned migrants. They had left Donegal in the early 1950s because of the lack of employment opportunities, and had lived in Scotland for 50 years with no intention of returning. Their family had settled in Scotland, but Sarah's husband had wanted to return in his old age to die in Donegal. They had returned with members of their family in 2005. I needed to confirm that they were indeed 'my Buchanans'. Sarah's family history tied in with mine, and she was able to give me the details of family burial plots and where the births, marriages and deaths were recorded. She knew that our both families were related to the American President James Buchanan.

Illustration 60   Buchanan burial ground in Ramelton old graveyard.

    Sarah Buchanan was an amazing source of information. She knew where Stony Batter was, and she knew about the Russells who had lived there. I was able to receive directions to the location from her.

Illustration 61   Stony Batter - Russell homestead.

Illustration 62   Stony Batter – Russell homestead

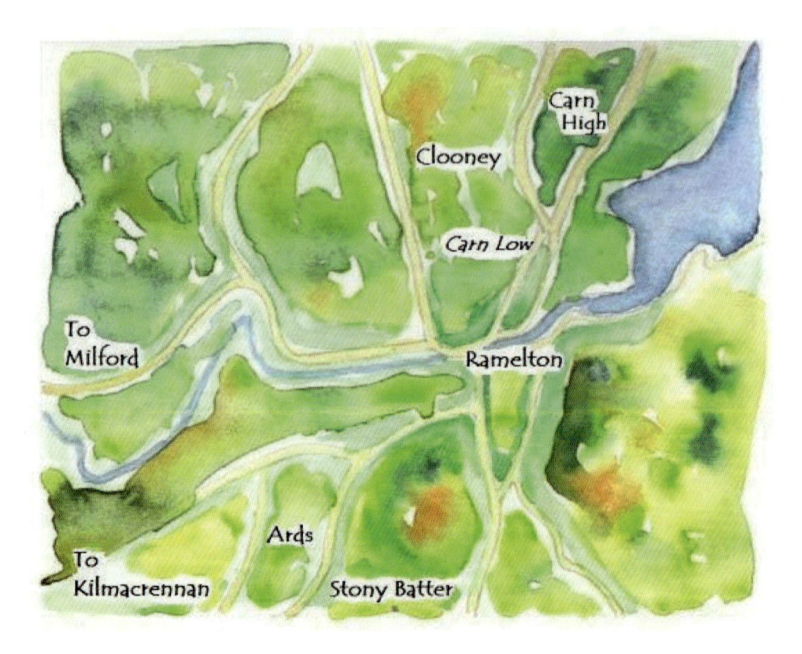

Map 22   Location of Carn High, Carn Low and Stony Batter [1]

THE SEARCH FOR OCCUPANTS OF STONY BATTER IN GRIFFITHS VALUATION 1848.

Map 23   Stony Batter, Ramelton [2]
Information from Ordnance Survey Ireland, Griffiths Valuation of Land 1848.

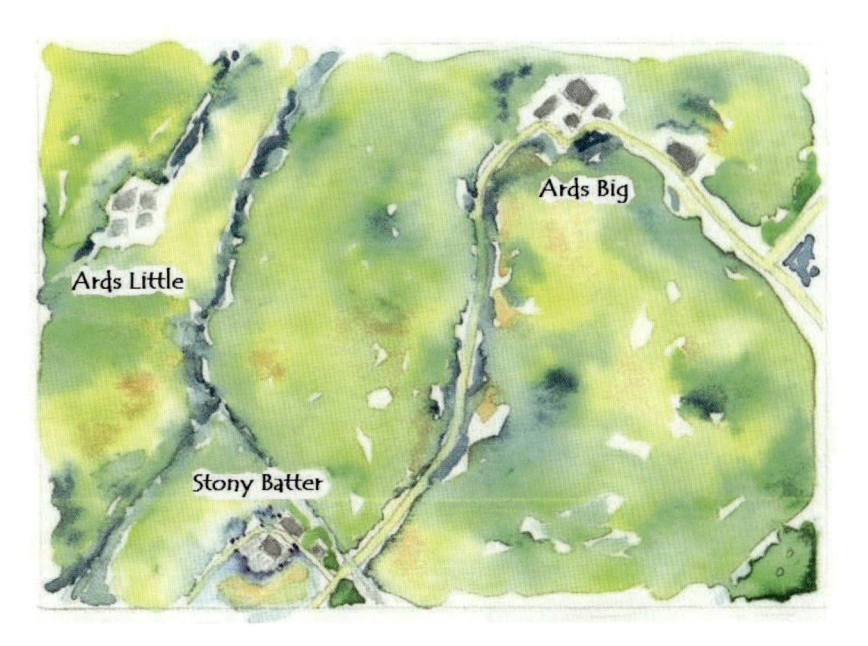

Map 24   Stony Batter, Ramelton, in relation to Ards Big and Ards Little

Information from Ordnance Survey Ireland, Griffiths Valuation of Land 1848.

THE FIRST SEARCH FOR OCCUPANTS OF ARDS BIG, IN GRIFFITHS VALUATION 1848

		ARDS, BIG. (Ord. S. 45.)			Total, .	179 0 22
1	a	James Watt,	Sir Jas. Stewart, Bart.,	Office and land,		27 1 18
-	b	Neal Dugary,	James Watt,	House and garden,		0 0 15
2		Florinda Watt,	Same,	House and garden,		0 1 35
3	a }	William Floyd,	Sir Jas. Stewart, Bt., {	House, offices, and land, Labourer's house,		62 1 5 —
4	A			Land,		·0 2 5
-	B			Land,		4 1 5
-	C	Samuel Floyd,	Same,	Land,		16 3 22
5	A a			House, offices, and land,		49 0 6
-	B			Land,		5 3 23
-	A b }			Cottier's house,		—
4	A a	Matthew M'Ilwain,	Samuel Floyd,	House,		—
5	B b	Richard M'Fadden,	Same,	House and garden,		0 0 20
6	A a }	John Aikin,	Sir Jas. Stewart, Bt., {	Offices and land, House, offices, and land.		104 3 35 1 1 10
-	A b	William Morrow,	John Aikin,	House,		—
-	c	Eliza Magrath,	Same,	House and garden,		0 0 20
-	d	Samuel Richey,	Same,	House, & small garden,		—
-	e	Andrew M'Connell,	Same,	Store,		—

Illustration 63   Occupants of Ards Big, Ramelton. [3]
Information from Ordnance Survey Ireland, Griffiths Valuation of Land.
Reproduced by permission of The Commissioner of Valuation, Ireland

I chose to begin the search in the townland of Ards Big, in Griffiths Valuation of Land.

Illustration 5 (OS 45) shows James Watt as occupant of 1(a) with offices and 27 acres of land in Ards. (It was known as Big Ards, locally, as there was also an Ards Little). There is also a tenant of 1(b) with a house and garden, which belongs to James Watt.

On the family scroll a Mary Watt is married to a Samuel Russell of Big Ards. They were the grandparents who cared for grandchildren James and John Buchanan on the death of their daughter Jane Russell, who had married John Buchanan, the children's father. There is also a Florinda Watt in Ards Big, the lands owned by Sir James Stewart. This search was unsuccessful in finding Samuel Russell, grandfather of James Buchanan who cared for him when he became an orphan.

These were the Watts of Ards Big, but Samuel Russell of the scroll is not mentioned. Yet my aunt distinctly said that they were well-to-do Church of Ireland farmers who lived there. Was there a marriage for consolidation of land?

THE SECOND SEARCH FOR OCCUPANTS IS IN THE TOWNLAND OF
DRUMBERN IN GRIFFITHS VALUATION 1848

		DRUMBERN. (Ord. S. 36.)					
1	a	Earl of Leitrim,	In fee,	Lime store and land,	3 .0 32	0 10
—	b	Patrick Harkin,	Earl of Leitrim,	House,	—	—
—	c	David & Samuel Watt,	Same,	Corn kiln, stores, & yard,	—	—
2		William Sweeney,	Same,	House, offices, and land,	12 2 16	5 5
3	a	Patrick Harkin,	Same,	House, offices, & land,	15 3 4	3 0
	b	Mandy Harkin,		House, office, & land,		3 0
4		Hugh Harkin,	Same,	House, offices, and land,	6 3 33	3 5
5		James M'Ginley,	Same,	House, offices, and land,	10 3 29	5 0
6		William Russell,	Same,	House, offices, and land,	11 3 3	0 0
7		James Larcus,	Same,	Land,	13 2 0	6 15
8		William Love,	Same,	Offices and land,	13 1 22	6 0
9		Patrick M'Gettigan,	Same,	Land,	2 3 26	1 0
10		Rev. Thomas Diver,	Same,	Land,	5 3 20	1 10
11		Samuel Russell,	Same,	House and land,	3 2 27	1 0
12	a	Joseph M'Carroll,	Same,	House and land,	2 3 20	1 0
	b			Pound (of no value),	—	—
—	c	John Buchanan,	Same,	House,	—	—
—	d	Mary Starrett,	John Buchanan,	House,	—	—

Illustration 64   Occupants of Drumbern, Ramelton. [4]
Information from Ordnance Survey Ireland, Griffiths Valuation of Land.

Reproduced by permission of The Commissioner of Valuation, Ireland.

On further examination of the records I found Samuel Russell in Drumbern townland in OS 36 in lands owned by Clements, the Earl of Leitrim. He had 3 acres. Samuel Russell (no 11) has a house and 3 acres of land. William Russell (no 6) has a house and offices and 11 acres of land. David and Samuel Watt (no 1c) have a Corn Kiln, stores and yard but no land. John Buchanan (12c) has a house which is rented out to Mary Starrett, and also a house in which he himself is a tenant. He has no land. The landlord in all these cases is Clements, the Earl of Leitrim. This confirms what my aunt had told me, that the landlord was the Earl of Leitrim, where John Buchanan had lived. However the connection between Big Ards and Samuel Watt had yet to be established.

In my earlier investigation of the tenants of the Carn on the lands of James Stewart, I had puzzled how Jane Russell and John Buchanan could have met and married. She was Church of Ireland and he was Presbyterian, so they would not have met through a Church affiliation. If he had been born in the Carn which is north of Ramelton, and she was in Big Ards, (as the locals called it), quite a distance south of Ramelton, what enabled them to meet? I realised when I looked at the Drumbern (OS 36) information, there were Buchanans, Russells and Watts in the same townland. I also realised that there was a link through marriage in a previous generation. Therefore they were related in some way. Samuel Russell who had 3 acres married Mary Watt in 1728, whose father had lands at Big Ards, according to the family scroll.

In the third search of the Freeholders in County Donegal in 1775, I found Samuel Russell, junior, of Big Ards. Samuel Russell senior had 3 acres in Drumbern, but now Samuel Russell junior had 27 acres at Big Ards. He must have acquired this land on his marriage to Mary Watt. This was the Church of Ireland couple who disapproved of their daughter Jane marrying John Buchanan in 1751 'a rough-necked Presbyterian' with no land to his name and only a house to live in and a house rented out.

THE FOURTH SEARCH FOR RUSSELL FREEHOLDERS IN BIG ARDS 1775

Russell,	Jno.	Upr. Cavan	Cavan	Gardiner	1768
	Jno.	Druminy	Druminy Upr.		
	Alexr.	Upr. Cavan		Gardiner	1768
	Petk.	Tullsmore		D. Chambers	1775
	Edwd.	do.		do.	1775
	Alexr.	Lignam		Gardiner	1775
	Jas.	do.		do.	1775
	Saml. junr.	Big Ards		Sir A. Stewart	1775
	Moses	Ellistren		H. Wray	1775

Illustration 65   Samuel Russell, Freeholder of Big Ards 1775 [5]
Reproduced by permission of PRONI

I had found the names that were on the scroll, and all the jigsaw seemed to fit together in the townland network, neighbourhood network, and marriage network. With regard to marriage among the descendants of original immigrants, from the information gathered, they were in the mode of planters marrying planters.

THE FIFTH SEARCH IS OF THE TOWNLANDS OF CARN LOW AND CLOONEY

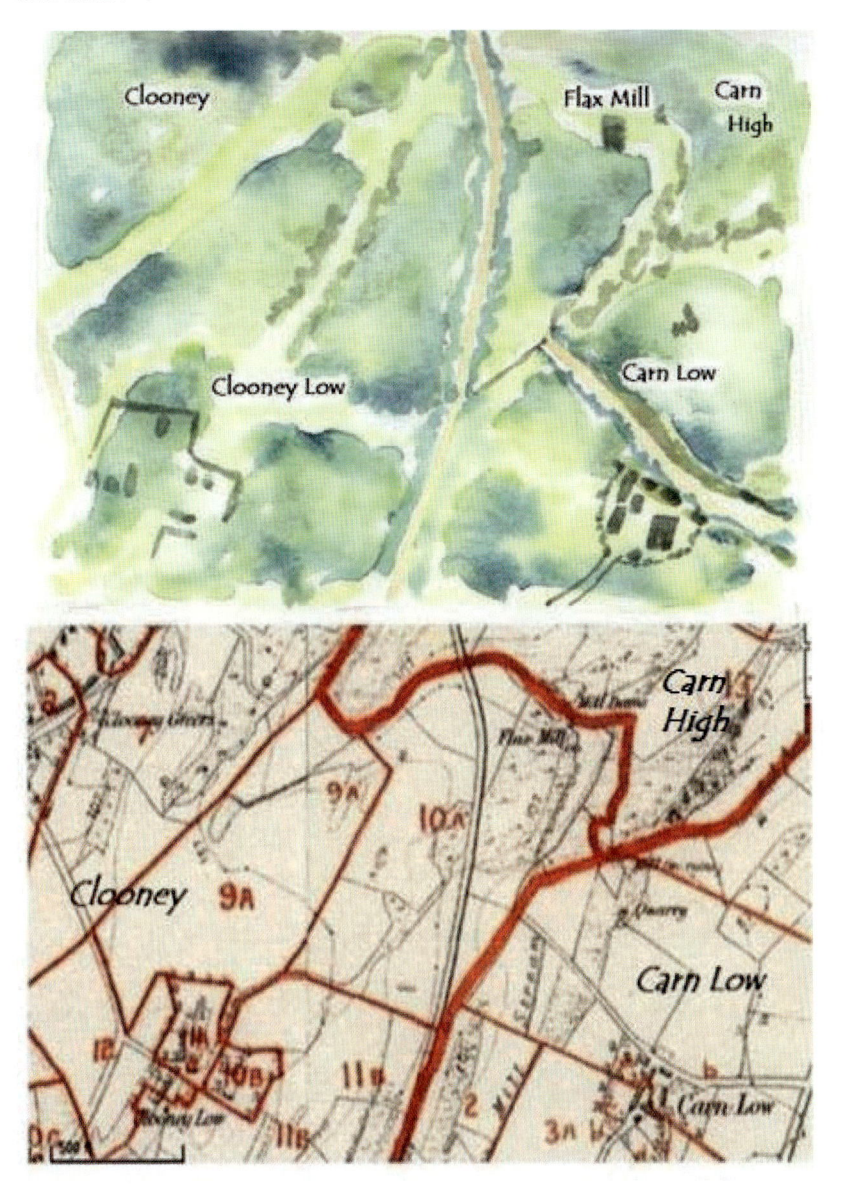

Map 25   Townlands of Carn Low and Clooney [6]

Reproduced by permission of The Commissioner of Valuation, Ireland [7] Information from Ordnance Survey Ireland, Griffiths Valuation of Land 1847 - 1864

SEARCH FOR OCCUPANTS OF CARN LOW, IN GRIFFITHS VALUATION 1848

		CARN, LOW. (Ord. S. 37 & 46.)					
1	a	Wm. Buchanan, sen.,	Sir Jas. Stewart, Bt.,	House, offices, & land,	89	3	0
	b	Wm. Buchanan, jun.,		House, offices, & land,			
-	c	Samuel Murray,	Wm. Buchanan, jun.,	House,	—		
-	d	James Coyle,	Wm. Buchanan, sen.,	House, office, & garden,	0	0	30
-	e	James Adams,	Wm. Buchanan, jun.,	House and garden,	0	0	30
-	f	Joseph Davis,	Same,	House and garden,	0	0	30
-	g	Elizabeth Buchanan,	Same,	House,	—		
-	h	Unoccupied,	Same,	House,	—		
2		David M'Clean,	John Fullerton,	House, offices, and land,	7	1	19
3	A			Land,	14	0	0
-	D	John Fullerton,	Sir Jas. Stewart, Bt.	House, offices, and land,	30	2	15
4	a & b			Flax-mill, off., and land,	41	3	3

Illustration 66   Occupants of Carn Low [8]
Reproduced by permission of The Commissioner of Valuation, Ireland

When I checked the occupants of Carn Low, in Griffiths Valuation 1848, I found in possession of 1(a) and 1 (b) were William Buchanan, senior, and William Buchanan, junior, with house, offices and 89 acres of land. Thomas Buchanan had migrated here from Deroran, County Tyrone around 1700. These were Buchanan descendants still in the same location.

From this I checked out the Freeholders Lists of 1761 for County Donegal. In 1761 there was a James Buchanan in the Carn, possibly the grandson of Thomas, and brother of John who had married Jane Russell of Big Ards. These were the occupants and freeholders of the land in Kearn (Cairn) and Cluney (Clooney) in 1761.

SEARCH FOR FREEHOLDER OCCUPANTS IN CAIRN AND CLOONEY, RAMELTON 1761

Buchannon, Jas.	Leatbegg	Clements	1761
Burgoyne, Rev. Thos.	Lifford	Ld. Erne	1761
Buchannon, Wm.	Lisnaness	H. Frey	1761
Jas.	Kearn	Sir A. Stewart	1761
John	Cluney	do.	1761

Illustration 67   Buchanan Freeholders 1761 in Cairn and Clooney [9]
Reproduced by permission of PRONI

From this information I decided that James Buchanan (phonetically spelled Buchannon), a Freeholder in Cairn (phonetically spelled Kearn) in 1761, on lands of Sir A. Stewart, was the closest relative in date that I could discover, to Thomas who migrated to the Carn from Deroran in 1700. The family scroll stated that William Buchanan of the Carn was the son of Thomas. John Buchanan (phonetically spelled Buchannon), a Freeholder in Clooney (phonetically spelled Cluney), may have also been a descendant of Thomas, and brother of James in Cairn in 1761.

I propose therefore that in Griffiths Valuation this William Buchanan senior, is the great grandson of Thomas Buchanan who was born in Deroran and moved to the Carn, Ramelton around 1700. James is the only Buchanan to hold land in the Carn in the Freeholders Poll Book of 1761. With regard to Jean Buchanan a cousin whom it is supposed Thomas married, there is a James Buchanan in Gorrowgart (Garrygort), which is north of Carn High, in the Hearth Rolls in 1665. Jean may have been his daughter. This is where my great grandparents 'White' Sam and his wife Rebecca lived.

So there would appear to be an integral connection between Buchanans who came over with the Plantation in the beginning of the 17th century with the Duke of Lennox. The list of the names of the family of William Buchanan (son of Thomas) of the Carn is as follows, in order of birth:

John b 1728 married Jane Russell of Big Ards (did not inherit Carn – may have migrated to the adjoining townland of Clooney or Cluney), or may have emigrated to America. My great grandfather was from this line through John's son Samuel born 1758.

William b 1730 (did not inherit the Carn – may have emigrated)

James b 1732 was the Freeholder listed for the Carn in 1761 and was father of William senior, and grandfather to William junior, in Griffiths 1848. President Buchanan visited here when he was Ambassador to Russia on his return journey in 1833 when William was the inhabitant of Carn.

George b 1733 (no record afterwards – may have emigrated)

Robert b 1734 (no record afterwards – may have emigrated)

Thomas b 1736 (no record afterwards – may have emigrated).

SEARCH FOR OCCUPANTS OF CLOONEY IN GRIFFITHS VALUATION 1848

		CLOONEY, (Ord. S 36, 37, 45, &46.)				
1 A		James Heron,				18 2 3
— B	a		Sir James Stewart, Bt.	House, offices, & land,		34 1 21
— c		John Heron,				11 0 37
—	A a	Archibald M'Ilwain,	James and John Heron,	House, off., & sm. garden,		—
—	B b	Unoccupied	James Heron,	House,		—
—	c	William Logan,	Same,	House & small garden,		—
—	d	Eliza Martin,	Same,	House and garden,		0 0 20
2	e	Archibald Stewart,	Same,	House and garden,		0 0 20
—	a	John Ellison,	Sir James Stewart, Bt.	House, offices, and land,		23 2 4
3	b	Robert Ellison,	John Ellison,	House,		—
4 A		Alexander Davis,	Sir James Stewart, Bt.	House, offices, and land.		20 3 3
— B	a	Richard Heron,	Same,	House, offices, & land,		29 0 25
—	b	John M'Naught,	Richard Heron,	House.		13 0 11
5	a	George Bond,	Sir James Stewart, Bt.	Caretaker's house & land.		—
0	b	Alexander Starrett, jun.	Same,	House, office, & garden,		0 1 0
7		David Grier,	Same,	House, offices, and land,		31 0 14
8		Robert Grier,	Same,	House, offices, and land,		32 2 5
—	a	Alexander Grier,	Same,	House, offices, and land,		30 3 5
9 A	b	James Cafferty,	Alexander Grier.	House,		—
— B		John Spencer,	Sir James Stewart, Bt.	Land,		13 0 18
10 A						6 3 31
— B		Walter Buchanan,	Same,	Flax-mill and land,		19 1 3
— c				House, offices, and land,		0 3 35
11 A	a			Land,		3 0 20

Illustration 68   Occupants of Clooney [10]
Reproduced by permission of The Land Commissioner, Ireland

This is the proof that Walter Buchanan was a Freeholder, in Clooney, as a grandson of John Buchanan, Freeholder, in 1761, and Flax grower in 1796. Walter had a flax-mill and 22 acres of land in 1848. It is from this line that Sarah Buchanan was descended. Her grandfather, John Buchanan migrated from the townland of Clooney to Carn High at the time of his marriage to Martha Davis, dressmaker, of Carn High. Sarah Buchanan knew that she shared a common ancestor with William's family of Carn Low.

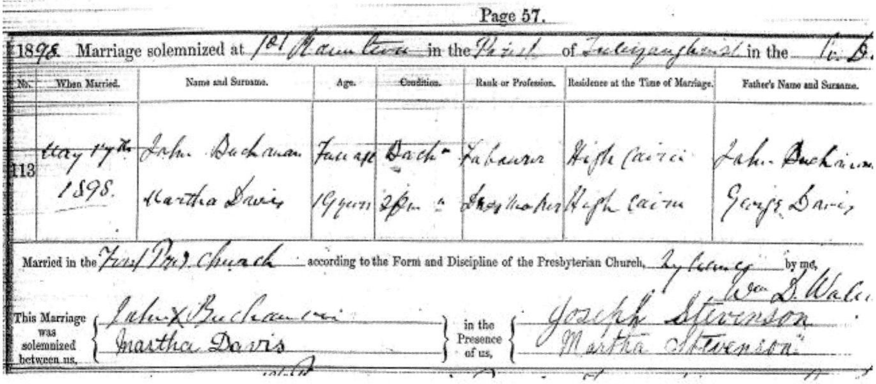
Page 57.

1898. Marriage solemnized at 1st Ramelton in the Parish of Tullyaughnish in the Co. D.

No.	When Married.	Name and Surname.	Age.	Condition.	Rank or Profession.	Residence at the Time of Marriage.	Father's Name and Surname.
113	May 17th 1898.	John Buchanan	Full age	Bach	Labourer	High Cairn	John Buchanan
		Martha Davis	19 years	Spin	Shopkeeper	High Cairn	George Davis

Married in the First Pres. Church according to the Form and Discipline of the Presbyterian Church, by me, Wm. D. Wallace

This Marriage was solemnized between us, John X Buchanan, Martha Davis; in the Presence of us, Joseph Stevenson, Martha Stevenson

Illustration 69 Marriage certificate of John Buchanan (born 1869 Clooney) and Martha Davis 1898 of High Cairn, Ramelton. Courtesy of Letterkenny Public Record Office

Many of these Buchanans of the Carn migrated to America, but there remained two descendants, who were brothers, at Carn Low in the 1920s, who died without issue, the last about 1927. A cousin, Mrs McCausland from Milford, was credited with making their wills helped by Mr Osborne, the solicitor in Milford. She inherited the land and sold it along with the rights of Tullydish for her benefit. With the proceeds she obtained land at Marble Hill, Dunfanaghy, and built the Shandon Hotel.[11]

Now that I had established that I was on the right trail, I had to locate original sources as evidence. Sarah Buchanan had confirmed that she was Presbyterian as were her father and grandfather before her. I began to plan my visit to the Public Record Office in Belfast to check the Church records to attempt to verify what she told me.

THE SEARCH OF RECORDS OF FIRST RAMELTON PRESBYTERIAN CHURCH, RAMELTON, CO. DONEGAL

1811	26/05/1814	Buchanan	Anne	Ramelton
1814	26/05/1814	Buchanan	James	Ramelton
1814	26/05/1814	Buchanan	William	Ramelton
1814	*26/05/1814*	*Buchanan*	*William*	*Clooney*
1814	26/05/1814	Buchanan	Nancy	Ramelton
1815	26/05/1814	Buchanan	Kitty	Ramelton
1819	*11/06/1819*	*Buchanan*	*Sally*	*Cluney*
1820	02/06/1820	Buchanan	Ann	Glenealy
1821	*01/06/1821*	*Buchanan*	*Mary*	*Cluney*
1821	01/06/1821	Buchanan	James	Ramelton
1822	01/06/1822	Buchanan	Hugh	Ramelton
1823	30/05/1823	Buchanan	Walter Jn	Ramelton
1823	*30/05/1823*	*Buchanan*	*Jane*	*Cluney*
1829	*01/06/1829*	*Buchanan*	*James*	*Cluney*
1829	*01/06/1829*	*Buchanan*	*Mary*	*Cluney*
1832	01/06/1832	Buchanan	Nancy	Ramelton
1835	01/06/1835	Buchanan	Catherine	Newtown
1835	*01/06/1835*	*Buchanan*	*Mary*	*Cluney*
1835	*01/06/1835*	*Buchanan*	*Walter*	*Cluney*
1835	*01/06/1835*	*Buchanan*	*William*	*Kairn* ☆
1836	*20/10/1836*	*Buchanan*	*William*	*Cluney*
1839	n.d.	*Buchanan*	*James*	*Clooney*
1839	n.d.	Buchanan	Nancy	Ramelton

Illustration 70 Young Communicants Rolls 1811-1839, Buchanans Courtesy of PRONI

Between 1811 and 1839 there were 23 young communicants enrolled. Children were enrolled as communicants generally when they reached their teenage years.

Ramelton town	10
Clooney or Cluney	10
Cairn or Carn	1
Glenealy	1
Newtown	1

This was evidence that there was a Buchanan family at Carn (Cairn, Kairn, Cairne) in the 1830s. They were Presbyterians. This evidence of the family at Carn is important because the family story included the recollection of James Buchanan, USA ambassador to Russia visiting Carn in 1833, to meet his Ramelton relatives on his way home from Russia. Mrs. John Buchanan (née Martha McNutt) of Garrygort who met him at Carn, corresponded with him in America, after the visit. The Buchanans at Garrygort were Covenanters, and there are descendants of this family who still worship in Milford Covenanter Church, County Donegal, to this day.

*Ramelton Quays courtesy of
http://www.donegalcottageholidays.com/towns/holiday-cottage-ramelton.php*

SUMMARY OF THE RESEARCH

George Buchanan of Blairlusk, Scotland, sold Blairlusk to his brother William and emigrated to Ireland in 1674. He settled in Deroran and married Elizabeth Mayne (born 1654), in 1675. His son Thomas migrated to Ramelton, County Donegal around 1700 and married a cousin Jean Buchanan. The story is that Thomas and his son William and five other sons, his grandson John and others, and numerous great grandsons emigrated to America and specifically Pennsylvania in the 18th century. Among them was James Buchanan who left for America in 1783. He was to become the father of President James Buchanan.

*Ramelton Quays courtesy of
http://www.donegalcottageholidays.com/towns/holiday-cottage-ramelton.php*

FROM IMMIGRATION OF GEORGE BUCHANAN 1674 FROM SCOTLAND

George of Blairlusk to Deroran

John of Tyrone	William of Tyrone	George of Munster	Thomas of Donegal
Born 1676	Born 1677	Born 1678	Born 1680
Deroran	Deroran	Deroran	Deroran

William (born son of Thomas Buchanan of Cairne, Ramelton, Co. Donegal) c1703

John Buchanan (Cairn) born c1725 married Jane Russell c1750 (John said to have gone to America - she was the daughter of Samuel Russell, Big Ards, Ramelton, and she was to follow him with the rest of the children). He possibly joined the army there, according to the story, or borrowed the wherewithal to buy land, maybe as an indentured person. She died when her youngest son was about 5 years old, around 1768. She never went to America with the rest of the family, because 'she had never heard from him'.

	Cairn			Stoney Batter	
Sarah	William	Samuel	Thomas	James	John
b 1753	b1755	b1758	b1759	b1761	b1763
m	m	m	went to USA	went to USA	m
Wm Morrison	Jane Pearse	Sarah Kirkwood	d s p	m Elizabeth Spear	
went to USA 1775					

Cairn	Cairn	Cairn	Garrygoct				
Samuel	James	John	John	Robert	Margaret	William	Jane
b1782	b1784	b1787	b1791	b1794	b1796	b1799	b1801
m			m	m no issue	m	m	m
Gallagher, Muross.			Martha McNutt		Wm Alcorn		

William 1835 (Presyterian communicants records)

William in Griffiths 1848

Illustration 71 George of Blairlusk to Deroran descended to William in Griffiths 1848

JAMES BUCHANAN BORN AT CARN, 1761 RAISED AS AN ORPHAN AT STONY BATTER, BIG ARDS – HIS EMIGRATION TO AMERICA 1783

The emigration of James Buchanan born 1761 at Carn - my first question was - when did James decide to go to America? He had obviously received the invitation by letter from his Uncle Joshua to go out there. However he would have had to find out the dates of the ships leaving Derry which was some distance away. He may have seen the advertisement for the ships departing from Derry in the Londonderry Journal. He may have heard the details from one of the shipping agents.

The story was that he sailed on the ship *Providence* on the 4th June 1783. It is also presumed that he knew that the American War of Independence was over, and that the time was right to travel. I found an advertisement for the ship Providence in the Londonderry Journal dated 28th April, 1783.[12]

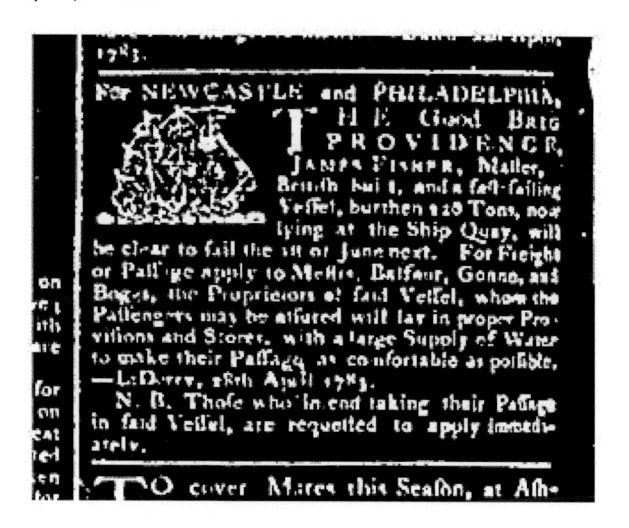

Illustration 72   Advertisement Courtesy of the Londonderry Journal

Or there could have been posters (similar to this one) giving information and agents who were usually to be found at the markets scouting for passengers for the next trip.

Illustration 73   Emigrant Ship Poster printed by Buchanan

According to Dickson (1966), most of the emigrants to colonial America left the north of Ireland through the ports of Londonderry, Portrush, Larne, Belfast and Newry.[13] He quotes from information in the Belfast Newsletter stating there were 422 vessels that sailed from these ports in the third quarter of the 18th century. The percentages quoted are 32.4% left from Belfast, 28.8% left from Londonderry, 19% left from Newry, 13% left from Larne, and 6.8% left from Portrush. He notes that 'several vessels called at two or more ports for emigrants'.

With reference to the copy of the advertisement in the Derry Journal on the 28th April 1783,[14] about the ship *Providence* sailing to Newcastle in the Delaware River, and onwards to Philadelphia, the date given for James Buchanan's departure is 4th June 1783.[15] Reference has already been made to Dickson's statistics on ships leaving the ports.

Another useful set of his statistics are the numbers of agents employed to scour the countryside for passengers to fill the emigrant ships. He selected the years 1750 – 1775 for a study of the out-agents.

He used the information from the newspapers in the different ports, for example the Belfast Newsletter and the Londonderry Journal. The two conclusions that he reached were that it would be inaccurate to suggest that all the emigrants who sailed from Belfast, for example, came from a limited area around Belfast. Out-agents ensured that people knew which ships were sailing from which port, the times of their sailings, and their destination ports, and the information was disseminated throughout the northern counties of Ireland.

The second conclusion that Dickson reached was that much of the emigration trade was in the hands of 'merchants cum ship-owners cum emigration agents,' [16] and he notes that one or more of the four Galt brothers 'was agent on twenty-four occasions'. These Coleraine brothers were 'part owners of the Providence and the Rainbow' [17] sailing vessels.

LEAVING IRELAND

How did James Buchanan feel as he was standing on the deck leaving Derry? The departure of the boat depended on the weather and the tides, so it might not have departed on the proposed date. The family story goes that his younger brother John drove James with his trunk in a horse and cart the 45 miles to the Ship Quay at Derry. The horse and cart was needed at Stony Batter so they probably had accommodation overnight in one of the local inns in Derry, and after the rest John would have returned home.

The following scene brought to mind something I had read about Rupert Brooke the poet, who, when leaving Liverpool for New York at the beginning of the twentieth century, felt terribly lonely because no one had come to see him off. Everyone else seemed to have friends. Excited groups of people surrounded him on every side. He alone was alone.

Looking down at the crowds who were waving, he noticed a dirty little boy – a street urchin. Quickly he ran down the gangway, found the boy and asked him, 'Will you wave to me if I give you a sixpence?' So he gave him a large handkerchief and the sixpence, and the poet returned to the ship. When the time came for the ship to set sail, the little boy waved furiously. Rupert Brooke said: 'I got my six penn'orth – and my farewell. I felt lonely no more.' Perhaps James felt lonely as like Rupert Brooke nobody was there to wave goodbye. Perhaps he was resigned to his fate, but maybe as a Christian believer, he would say that resignation is surrender to fate, but acceptance of his destiny was surrender to God, and to the destiny God had planned for him in the Promised Land.

THE JOURNEY ACROSS THE ATLANTIC

An article in The Belfast Newsletter, Tuesday, 7 July 1767 gives a very good description of what the ship was like in which James Buchanan travelled.

> 'The ship Providence, Captain Clark of Coleraine, which some time ago sailed from Portrush arrived safely at Newcastle, America after a passage of six weeks and three days with upwards of 300 passengers on board.' [18]

Another article in The Belfast Newsletter, perhaps on the arrival on the return journey states:

> 'The Ship PROVIDENCE, 300 Tons, Captain Thomas Clarke, will sail from Portrush on the first of August next. Those who incline to go in this ship as Passengers, Redemptioners, or Servants, or have goods to Ship on Freight, are desired to apply to Messrs John and Charles Galt, or Alexander Lawrence of Coleraine, Merchants; or to Messrs John Boyd, John Caldwell junior, or James Reilly of Ballymoney Merchants; or to Capt. Clarke either of whom will agree on reasonable Terms. Capt. Clarke has been in this Trade long and he likes to live regularly well himself, so is he equally careful that everyone in his ship shall do so likewise.' Coleraine 22nd June, 1767.[19]

A SAFE ARRIVAL WAS NOT ALWAYS GUARANTEED.

An example of what some passengers might experience on such a Transatlantic Crossing is revealed in The Belfast News Letter, 6 January 1769.

Illustration 74   The journey - some had problems

'Safe Arrival of Passengers Belonging to Ship Providence, at New York'.

> The passengers of the Providence gave the following account, viz. 'That the said ship Providence sailed from Coleraine the 27th of August, and on the 8th of September, in Lat. 45, 60, Long. 34, sprung a leak, which gained so fast upon her, that with both pumps and bailing they could scarce keep her above water, so that on the 12th they were obliged to take to their boats, the above 13 in the long-boat, and 4 to the yawl, being all they could hold; 19 other passengers and seamen chose to stay in the ship rather than risk perishing sooner in the boats; the two boats parted, and the long-boat, after having quitted the ship eight days, happily fell in with Capt. Cowan, who has safely landed there all the people that were in her.' [20]

THE NUMBER OF SHIPS LEAVING NORTHERN IRELAND FOR AMERICA

In the Londonderry Journal dated Friday 9th April 1775 the following article highlighted the reaction to the emigration of the people.

> 'It may be supported on a moderate computation that the number of Passengers was equal to the tons. The greatest part of these Emigrants paid their passage, which at £3-10s. each, amounted to 60,725 Pounds. Most of them people employed in the Linen Manufacture, or Farmers, and of some property which they turned into money and carried with them: [In evidence of this, it was computed that one ship, last year, had no less than 4000L. in specie on board.] Their removal is forcibly felt in this country. This prevalent humour of industrious Protestants withdrawing from this once flourishing corner of the kingdom seems to be increasing: and it is thought the number to be considerably larger this year, than ever.'

> 'The North of Ireland has been occasionally opposed to emigration, for which the American settlements have been much beholden: But till now, it was chiefly the very meanest of the people that went off, mostly in the station of indented servants and such as had become obnoxious to their mother Country. In [those?] it is computed from many concurrent circumstances, that the North of Ireland has in the last five or six years been drained of one fourth of its trading [cash?], and the like proportion of the manufacturing people. Where the [evil?] will end, remains only in the womb of time to determine'. [21]

According to Dickson, the details of numbers of ships are as follows:

In 1771 there were :

13 Passenger ships sailed from Londonderry 3650 tons.
7 Passenger ships sailed from Belfast 1751 tons.
9 Passenger ships sailed from Newry 2800 tons.
1 Passenger ship sailed from Portrush 250 tons.
2 Passenger ships sailed from Larne 450 tons.

In 1772 there were :

9 Passenger ships sailed from Londonderry 2650 tons.
10 Passenger ships sailed from Belfast 2650 tons.
5 Passenger ships sailed from Newry 1600 tons.
1 Passenger ship sailed from Portrush 250 tons.
5 Passenger ships sailed from Larne 1300 tons.

In 1771 passengers about 9101
In 1772 passengers about 9450
The greatest part of these emigrants paid their passage to America which was £3.10s. per head.

It was not possible to obtain similar information nearer the time James Buchanan emigrated to America in 1783. The fact was that he was 22 years old, and the American War of Independence was over. He had an offer of a new life with a job and accommodation in Pennsylvania. To date I have not been able to find the record of the arrival of the *Providence* in Philadelphia. The records were not being kept so accurately in the year 1783, the year the war ended. A new jurisdiction was now in place. However it is obvious that according to the advertisement in the Londonderry Journal in April of 1783 the ship Providence existed, and was intending to sail. It is also obvious that James Buchanan arrived in America. So it is assumed that the information on the family scroll was correct.

ARRIVAL AT PHILADELPHIA, PENNSYLVANIA

Illustration 75   Delaware River - Penn's Landing at Philadelphia 18 th century.

Illustration 76   Penn's Landing at Philadelphia 18 th century.

Illustration 77   Arriving from Ireland

Sculpture depicted the Irish arriving in Philadelphia at Penn's Landing in the mid C19th, by Glenna Goodacre.

JAMES BUCHANAN'S ARRIVAL IN AMERICA 1783.

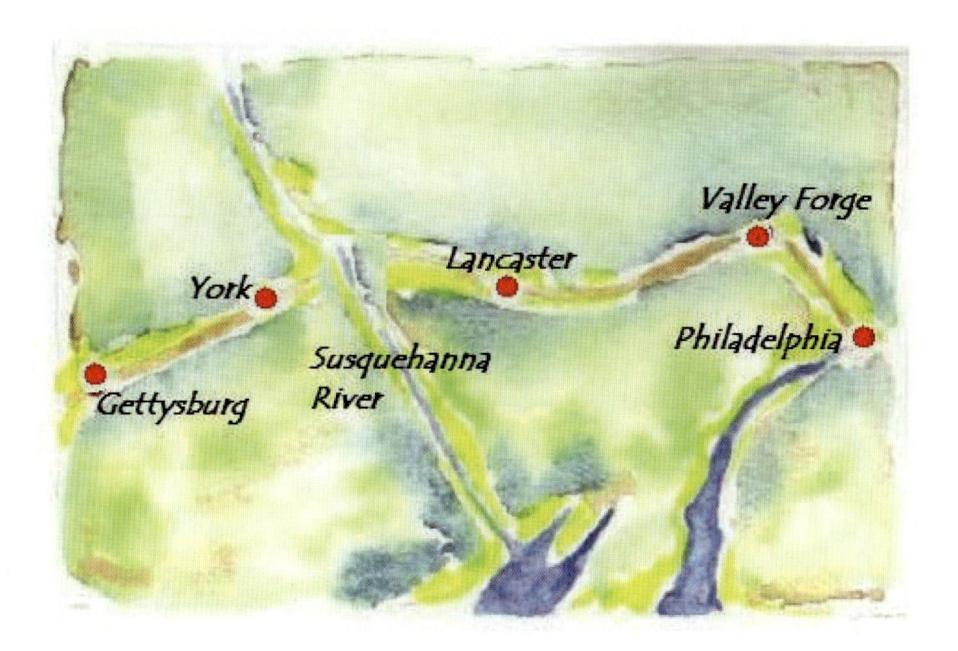

Map 26   From Philadelphia to Gettysburg 1783

  According to the family story Uncle Joshua Russell met his nephew James Buchanan at Penn's Landing in Philadelphia with two horses. They rode out of Philadelphia and their first stop was at Valley Forge, a distance of about 24 miles. Their route was via Lancaster, a distance of 75 miles from Valley Forge. They continued via York, 104 miles from Lancaster. Then from York they travelled to Gettysburg which was a distance of 118 miles. In total the journey was about 321 miles, and for Uncle Joshua it had been the round trip. 'Joshua had been a wagon-master on this road carrying flour from York to the starving Continental Army.'[22]   He knew the road very well.

  I had decided to follow the migrant James Buchanan's footprints, not on a horse, but in a campervan. I eventually reached Gettysburg and was able to start locating the people and places that had been spoken of in the story. Did Russell's Tavern still exist on the Huntersburg Road outside Gettysburg? Nobody I asked knew about a Huntersburg Road, but they did know of a Russell Tavern Road out of Gettysburg.

THE SEARCH FOR RUSSELL'S TAVERN, GETTYSBURG

Illustration 78   Sign for Russell Tavern Road

CHAIN MIGRATION

The search for Joshua Russell, uncle of James Buchanan began. In the archives of Adams County Historical Society, Gettysburg, I found a petition from Samuel Russell for a Tavern at Hunterstown Road, Gettysburg, dated 1806, to Adams County Court. I realised that this was an example of extended family chain migration. Samuel Russell was the son of Joshua Russell, brother of James Buchanan's mother, Jane Russell. Samuel Russell was James Buchanan's cousin. His father Joshua Russell (1750–1807) died 5 January 1807 when he was fifty-seven years old. Joshua had owned the Tavern. I found a petition to Adams County Court dated May 1806 from his son Samuel petitioning 'to grant a licence to keep a house of public entertainment'. It was addressed to the Honourable James Hamilton Esquire requesting that he would recommend him to His Excellency the Governor for this licence.

Illustration 79   Petition to Adams County Court by Samuel Russell
Courtesy of Adams County Historical Society

Illustration 80   Russell's Tavern, Gettysburg [23]

Illustration 81   Russell's Tavern, Gettysburg

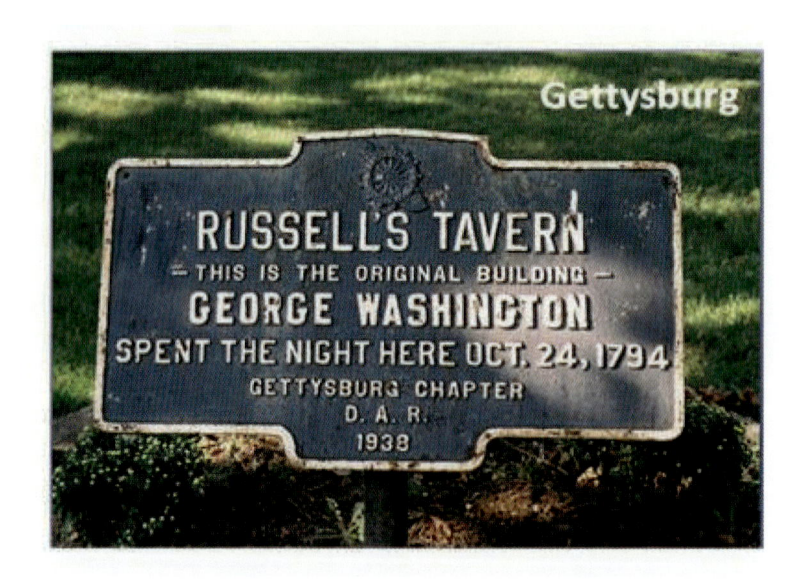

Illustration 82   Close-up of the notice in the garden at the front

THE SEARCH FOR JOSHUA RUSSELL

To progress the search for Joshua Russell I decided to investigate the land warrants and patents.

LAND WARRANTS IN YORK AND ADAMS COUNTIES, PENNSYLVANIA [24]
I found a Land Warrant in York County: Survey A- 411

STRABANE – BUTLER TOWNSHIPS
York Warrant Register: R – 145
WARRANT – West Side Application No 5590,

August 30, 1769, 30 acres to Joshua Russell.

March 28, 1775, 275 acres to Joshua Russell

SURVEY – January 13, 1770, 299 acres 80 perches to Joshua Russell;

(Author's note: Survey D-64-297 notes that the West Side Application was for the 84 acre tract, Russell bought the 217 acre tract at a sheriff's sale. The previous settler is not known. Contiguous earlier dated surveys note a Joshua Russell occupying this tract as early as 1762.)[25]

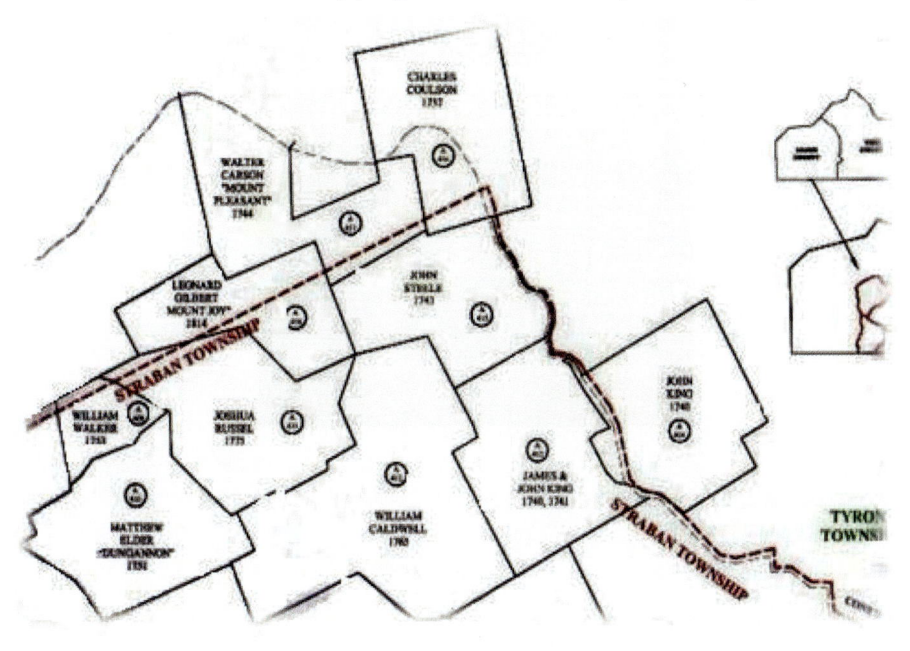

Map 27 Joshua Russell tract of land, Straban Township, Manor of Maske, Adams County. Courtesy of Adams County Historical Society.[26] Used by permission of Neal Otto Hively.

These facts helped to establish that Joshua Russell had existed and had owned property and land in the Gettysburg area.

119

GETTSYSBURG PRESBYTERIAN CHURCH RECORDS

The next task was to establish if Joshua Russell had belonged to a local church. A record of a report that he had fought in the American Revolutionary War was found in the records of Blacks Presbyterian Graveyard, Gettysburg.

> 'Joshua Russell (1750–1807) died 5 January 1807 when he was fifty-seven years old. The proprietor of 'Russell Tavern', Mr Russell was the uncle of the father of President James Buchanan.[27]

I made a search of Black's Graveyard and found Joshua Russell's gravestone.

Illustration 83   Black's Graveyard

Illustration 84   Gravestone of Joshua Russell

Illustration 85   Location of Joshua Russell's gravestone dated 1807 in Black's Graveyard (fourth up on the left next to the fence)

'The church was of great importance and guided their lives,' [28]

CONCLUSION FROM THIS RESEARCH ON JOSHUA RUSSELL

The conclusion reached about Joshua Russell, the maternal uncle of James Buchanan, is that the family scroll did record a true course of events. He really did exist and he had emigrated to America, had become successful in acquiring Russell's Tavern at Gettysburg, Pennsylvania, for which the entertainment licence had been granted later to his son Samuel. Joshua Russell also acquired lands in the district of Gettysburg. He was a member of the Russell family chain migration which also included the Buchanan family of the Cairn (Carn), Ramelton, through Jane Russell the mother of James Buchanan.

Joshua Russell belonged to Gettysburg Presbyterian Church established on the site of the old Black's Graveyard (named after its first minister) in 1740. In the records of the church it was stated that he served in the Revolutionary War, and that he was an uncle of James Buchanan who was the father of President Buchanan. The story about his uncle Joshua sending for James because 'he was good at figures' was true. He did meet him off the boat at Philadelphia. He did go and work for his uncle Joshua for a time until he purchased his own trading post some time later.

THE LINK BETWEEN THE RUSSELLS AND THE BUCHANANS

Also buried in Gettysburg graveyard is Robert Buchanan. This man would have been related to James Buchanan 'the emigrant' of 1783 from Stony Batter, Ramelton. In a chart giving the lineage of the descendants of 'William of County Tyrone' who died in 1725, brother of Thomas the internal migrant to Ramelton and emigrant to Pennsylvania, there is a note about William's son Robert. It states that:

> 'Robert Buchanan was born in County Tyrone in 1696/7. He came to Pennsylvania in 1720 and died near Marsh Creek. His tombstone is at Gettysburg, having been removed from the cemetery at Marsh Creek located in Cumberland County. Jane Boyd (his wife) gave bond as Admix 02-11-1748/9 in amount of 300 Pounds to William Buchanan and Hance Hamilton. Jane died in January 1779 at an advanced age.' [29]

Here is proof that Buchanans had emigrated in the early 1700s from Deroran, County Tyrone, which is recorded in the family scroll.

Further proof comes from a Genealogy magazine published in 1899.

'There was quite a large immigration to Pennsylvania of persons bearing the surname of Buchanan between the years of 1720 and 1776, almost all of them being related to each other. They all appear to have removed from the north of Ireland (principally from Tyrone and Donegal) and were Scotch Irish Presbyterians.' [30]

'Robert Buchanan of Tyrone took up a part of an eight hundred acre tract of land on the Conondoguinet, near the mouth of Silver's Run. Robert Buchanan had several brothers in Pennsylvania then: One Walter, who lived at East Pennsborough, Cumberland County, where Robert removed, and William, who kept an inn at Carlisle in 1753, and another brother who resided in Hopewell Township in 1748. There were four, if not six, brothers who came to Pennsylvania from 1724 to 1730.'

'Robert, the eldest of the brothers, was born in Tyrone 1696/7 and died in Lancaster County in 1748. He settled first in the township of Donegal, Chester County, before 1725, where he held considerable lands. Robert Buchanan was a man of considerable education, and his letters, a few which are extant, are superior to many of his time. The records show so many transactions in land that it is difficult, if not impossible, to state positively where he resided during all the twenty-five years he lived in Pennsylvania. He died upon a farm near the Marsh Creek settlement and was buried in the Presbyterian Church ground near Gettysburg.' [31]

In another document on Pennsylvania Genealogy including the history of York County, I found a Robert and William Buchanan who were early settlers in 1718, in Donegal Township. In the history of York County (p739) in Lower Chanceford Township there is a William Buchanan with 233 acres and 7 persons, a John Buchanan with no acres and 3 persons, a John Buchanan senior, with 150 acres and 9 persons. On page 757 in Fawn Township there is a James Buchanan with 200 acres and a Samuel Buchanan with 310 acres.

All of these migrants were also found in Hazard's Volume of Buchanans in Pennsylvania.[32] In the 1790 Index to heads of families I counted 49 Heads of Buchanan families in Pennsylvania.[33]

In another search of the pensions from the American Revolutionary War I found one person named John Buchanan. The details are as follows:

John Buchanan enlisted in Fannett Township, Cumberland (later Franklin) County, Pennsylvania, in June 1778. He served as a private in Captain Isaac Miller's Company, Colonel Daniel Brodhand's Pennsylvania Regiment, and in Captains Morgan's and Thomas Farrel's Companies 13th Virginia Regiment. He went on General McIntosh's Western campaign and was discharged June 14, 1779. His discharge was signed by Colonels Richard Campbell and Daniel Brodhead. He was allowed pension on his application executed April 2, 1818, at which time he was a resident of Fannett Township, Franklin County, Pennsylvania. He was aged 69 years in 1820. He died February 4, 1826. There are no data as to his family.[34]

I had obviously not found John Buchanan who had married Jane Russell in Donegal, Ireland, and who was the father of James Buchanan the emigrant. In the family story John had disappeared and it was said that he had gone to America and joined the Revolutionary Army. It is interesting that the comment on the pension slip includes the fact that there is no data on his family. However if John Buchanan gave his age as 69 in 1820 then he must have been born in 1751 and could not have been the father of James Buchanan who was the second youngest son of the marriage, born 1761. This search had been unsuccessful in finding John Buchanan, the grand-father of the President. The search in the Pennsylvanian records is still ongoing.

CHAIN MIGRATION IN LAND WARRANTS AND PATENTS

York County was part of Lancaster County until October 1749.

In further searches of Pennsylvania Archives 3rd S., Vol. XXIV, I found early warrantees as follows between 1737 and 1750 [35] showing Chain Migration or linked migration over a period of 13 years.

James Buchanan	400 acres	Jan 17, 1737
Samuel Buchanan	200 acres	Apr 25, 1737
Robert Buchanan	425 acres	Apr 10, 1741
Robert Buchanan	210 acres	Jan 13, 1742
Thomas Buchanan	150 acres	Mar 20, 1743
George Buchanan	50 acres	Apr 24, 1746
George Buchanan	60 acres	Apr 24, 1746
Robert Buchanan	300 acres	May 31, 1746
Richard Buchanan	50 acres	Aug 30, 1746
James Buchanan	60 acres	Sep 25, 1748
James Buchanan	50 acres	Nov 28, 1748
Richard Buchanan	50 acres	Sep 25, 1750

Of particular interest is Thomas Buchanan who is listed as a warrantee for 150 acres on March 20, 1743. Was he the Thomas Buchanan who was the youngest son of George Buchanan of Deroran, Co. Tyrone, who was the great-great-grandfather of the President? Thomas had migrated to Ramelton and it is believed he subsequently emigrated to America, where he acquired lands in Pennsylvania, as did his son William Buchanan of Carn, Ramelton. I wondered how they managed to acquire land when they arrived in America.

HOW DID THE EMIGRANTS ACQUIRE LAND IN PENNSYLVANIA?

I found a warrant for land for John Buchanan in York County. Perhaps he was the husband of Jane Russell who had gone to America and not been heard from since. I decided to search the land records. I did not understand the terms being used. What was a land warrant, or all the other terms used in the land records?

The State Land Records of Pennsylvania give the following definitions of the five stages in the acquisition of land in Pennsylvania.

Application – a request for a warrant to have a survey made, usually a slip of paper.

Warrant – a certificate authorising a survey of a tract of land; initiates title of a property and provides the basis for legal settlement, but does not convey all rights to the property.

Survey – sketch boundaries of tract of land with exact determination of total acreage.

Return – verbal description of property boundaries; the wording is similar to that of a patent; an internal document sent from Surveyor General to Secretary of the Land Office.

Patent – final official deed from the Penns or the Commonwealth, which conveys clear title and all rights to the private owner.

If the land was purchased before 1733 I searched the Patent Indexes. If the land was purchased after 1733 I searched the Warrant Registers by county.[36]

Penn also deeded lands to the church. In 1740 deeds of land for 200 acres were signed to the Donegal church by William Penn.[37]

Most of the Scots-Irish settled in and around Lancaster, on arrival in Pennsylvania, in the early 18th century. Then, as land became available, they continued the drift westward. Once a crossing had been established over the Susquehanna River they pushed hard towards the Allegheny Mountains. The Buchanans were there amongst them. I decided to choose the location, Donegal, in Lancaster County, and follow some of these internal migrants migrating west.

'By the mid 18th Century 12,000 Scots-Irish were coming to America each year. Most of the early settlers were Scots who had been relocated to Ulster, around Donegal and Derry, from where they emigrated to America. By 1722 those arriving in the Susquehanna River area chose their land for settlement and named the area Donegal.' [38]

In 1714 emigration of Scots-Irish to the Susquehanna Valley began and in 1732 the Presbytery of Donegal Presbyterian Church was organised. This is a definite pattern that I have observed in most of the research. The settlers built a log dwelling, and together they built a log church building as soon as possible afterwards.

Illustration 86   Donegal Presbyterian Church, Susquehanna River Valley, Lancaster County

The story surrounding the Donegal Church itself is that during divine service in 1777 an express rider rode up to the church bringing the news that General Howe was preparing to invade Pennsylvania. He engaged Captain Lowry, who was attending the service, to re-organise his men to defend themselves. The congregation gathered around the Witness Tree and joined hands and prayed – they then pledged allegiance to the cause for Independence.

Illustration 87   Donegal Presbyterian Church, Lancaster County

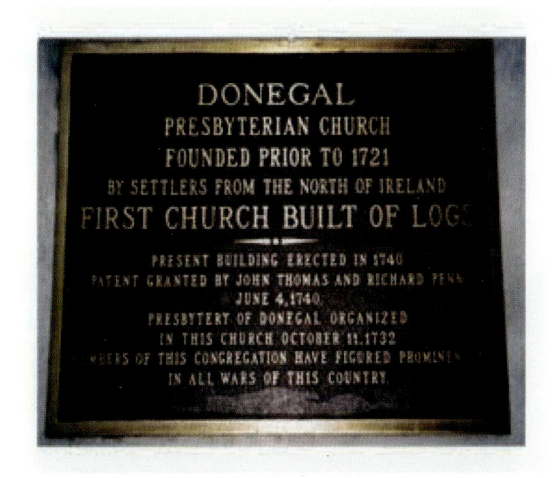

Illustration 88   Donegal Church Notice, Lancaster County

From the history of the Donegal church I learned that in the summer of 1740 the Presbytery of Donegal began to provide preaching for Presbyterians who had settled along Marsh Creek, and took steps to organise a church. Marsh Creek was due west and I decided to make some enquiries there.[39]

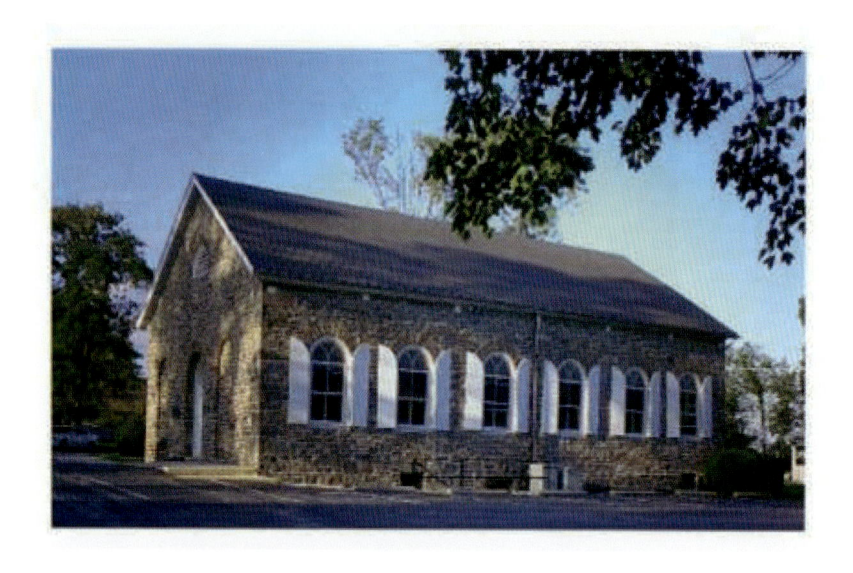

Illustration 89   Lower Marsh Creek Presbyterian Church

Illustration 90   Lower Marsh Creek Presbyterian Church Sign

   This may well have been the location of the original church where James Buchanan was married to Elizabeth Speer as these graves are belonging to the Speer family, who lived at North Mountain, close by. They had migrated here from the Susquehanna Valley area. They were called Robert and Jane Speer.

Illustration 91   Gravestones of the parents of Elizabeth Speer, wife of James Buchanan

Now that I had found the gravestones of Robert and Jane Speer, the parents of Elizabeth Speer, I knew that the evidence for the Land Patent for James Buchanan of Stony Batter was further west than Gettysburg or Lower Marsh Creek. I searched for Stony Batter and found it under the Patent of John Tom. The family story was that James Buchanan had heard of a trading post needing someone to run it and he had left Russell's Tavern and had gone west to Cove Gap to work there.

THE SEARCH FOR JAMES BUCHANAN AMONG THE DISTRIBUTION OF LAND BETWEEN THE IMMIGRANT SETTLERS

William Penn had been granted Pennsylvania – 'Penn's Woods' in 1681. The first people to live in this area of the wilderness were fur traders. According to Gerald Lestz, John Kennedy was the first person to receive a Penn deed for land that is now in Lancaster County. This was in the Eastern Section in 1691. The Mennonites, fleeing persecution, made the first permanent settlement in 1710. The Amish arrived not long afterwards. Lancaster was established in 1730 and given its name by John Wright, and was settled by the English and Germans.

Penn ensured that the 'fierce Scots-Irish Presbyterians' were on the borders west, north and south of Lancaster. It became a jumping off ground for all those who wished to travel west to the wilderness.[40] Gettysburg was located in the Manor of Maske.[41] Many Scots-Irish immigrants settled in and around this area.

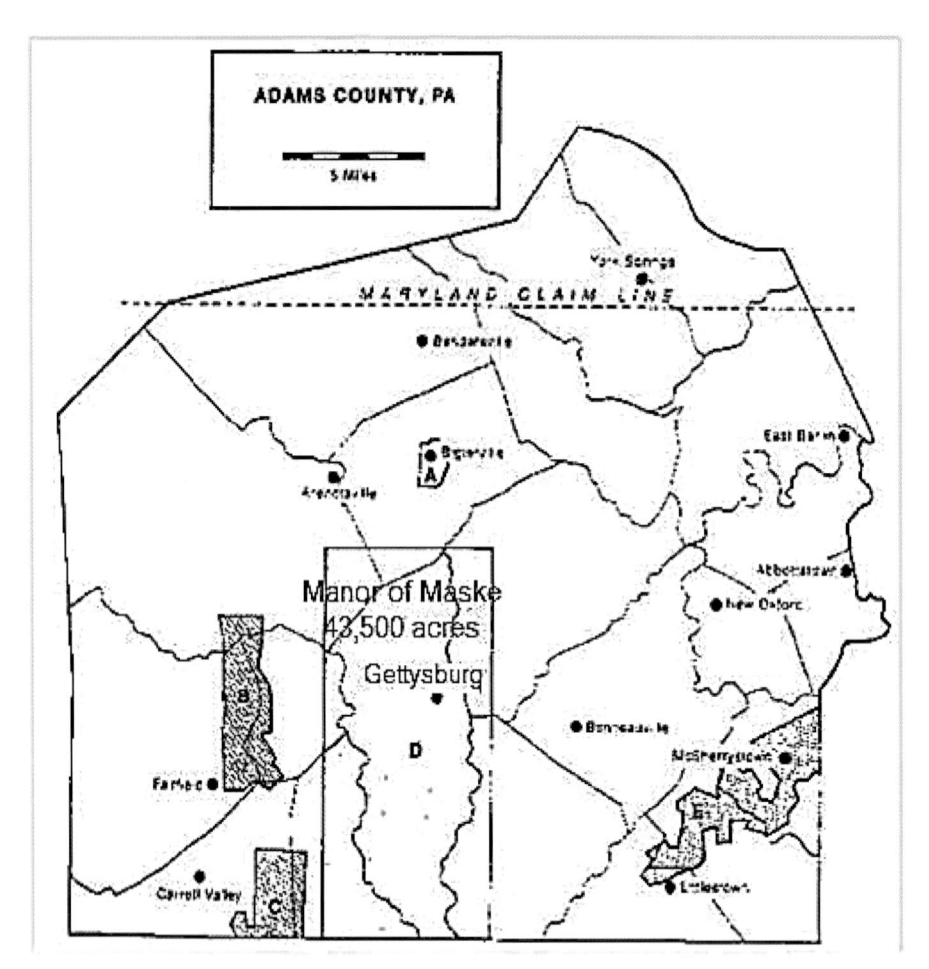

Illustration 92   The Manor of Maske
By permission of Neal Otto Hively.

　　　I searched The Manor of Maske - 43,500 acres, which is one of the various manors set aside by the Penn family as their private preserves, along with Possum Creek Manor, in Adams County. I did not find Stony Batter or James Buchanan.

Illustration 93   Manor of Maske wall plaque

THE SEARCH FOR JAMES BUCHANAN AND STONY BATTER

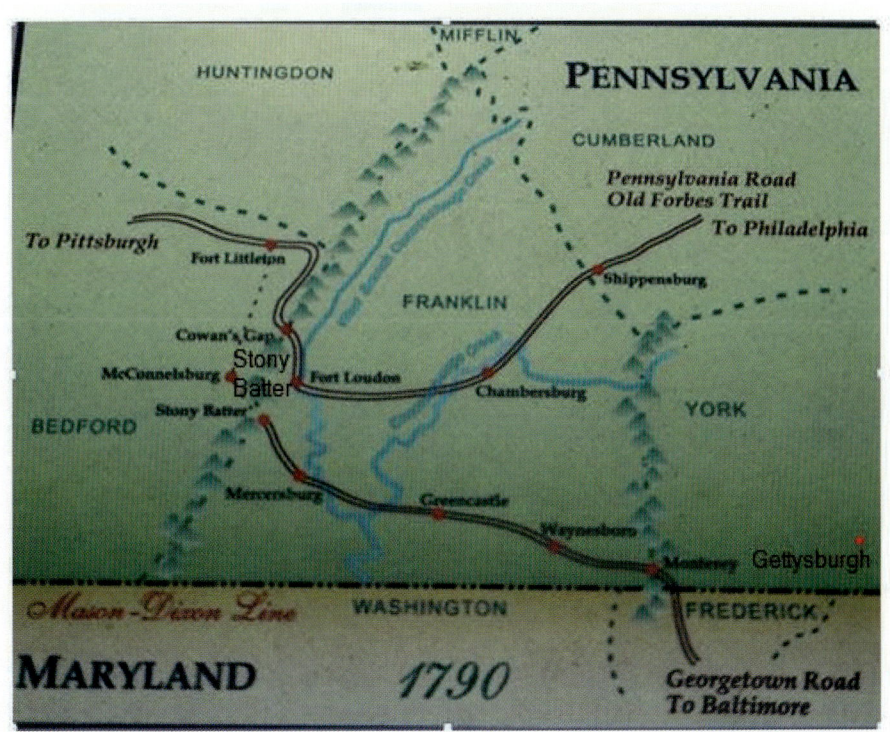

Map 28   Map of the Pennsylvania Road to Philadelphia showing Stony Batter

I found this old map of 1790 on a road sign which showed the road to Stony Batter, and which was clearly marked on the map. Stony Batter had been in Franklin County before Adams County had been carved out of Franklin County. The area was known as Cove Gap, in the Allegheny Mountains. James Buchanan had given the land at Cove Gap the name of Stony Batter, named after his grandparents Russell's home place in Ramelton, County Donegal, Ireland. While John Tom owned it, it was known as Cove Gap trading post.

SURVEY OF COVE GAP FOR JOHN TOM AND WARRANT GRANTED TO HIM FOR 61 ACRES ON 1 FEB 1786. [42]

Warrant granted to John Tom bearing the date 01 February 1786. [43]

OLD MAP LOCATION OF STONY BATTER, COVE GAP.

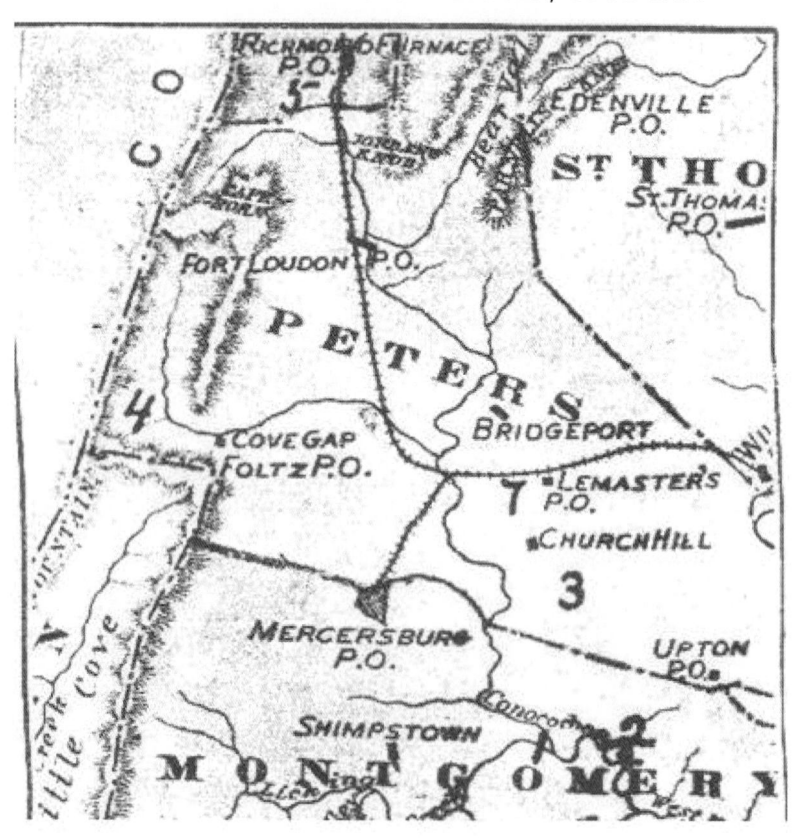

Map 29   Location of Cove Gap, N.W. of Mercersburg
Source – 'Old Mercersburg, PA' by Women's' Club of Mercersburg, 1949

WHO WAS JOHN TOM?

'John Tom served 1780-81 under Capts. James Patton, Robert Dickey and Thomas McDowell. In February 1785, he was granted a tract of 100 acres, including his improvement at the foot of Cove Mountain. In 1786, John Tom and wife, Jane, sold it to James Buchanan, 100 acres for 200 pounds in Cove Gap, also all the dwelling houses, store houses, stables and all other appurtenances, "where the said Tom now lives on." This is undoubtedly the tract on which Pennsylvania's only President was born.' James Buchanan, (the emigrant) was later to become the father of James Buchanan the President.[44] This was the proof I needed. Leading on from this information, in a further search I found the following account:

'After a year as Tom's helper, Buchanan got the chance to buy the Stony Batter property. Legend long had it that this transaction involved some sharp practice, but the court records show only that on December 15, 1786, John Tom offered to sell his property to Buchanan for 200 pounds, Pennsylvania currency, promising in the contract that the land was "free of all Taxes, Debts, dues or demands". A few days after Buchanan had recorded these terms of sale, however, John Ferguson of Chambersburg sued Tom for over 500 pounds owing to him and guaranteed by the property. The December County Court confirmed this judgment against Tom, and the February Court ordered a sheriff's sale of Stony Batter, the proceeds to go to Ferguson. Buchanan bought the 100-acre tract for 142 pounds at the public sale on June 23, 1787.'[45]

In all it had cost him 342 pounds.

Illustration 94   The Buchanan Trading Post at Stony Batter
Courtesy of Ramelton library, County Donegal, Ireland

THE SEARCH AMONG CHURCH RECORDS FOR JAMES BUCHANAN

EARLY GUINSTON PRESBYTERIAN CHURCH FAMILIES:

I found early settlers Buchanan, Russell and Speer among the members of the Guinston Presbyterian Church families located just west of the Susquehanna River, in the church records. These same names appeared further west later in the century.

Guinston Tracts of Land	Year and Survey Tract [46]	
William Buchanon	1774	C-369, 370
John Buchanon	1775	C-388, 387
John Russel	1775	Windsor
James Spear	1775	C-271

THE SEARCH AMONG UPPER WEST CONCOCHEAGUE PRESBYTERIAN CHURCH RECORDS, MERCERSBURG, PENNSYLVANIA FOR JAMES BUCHANAN.

The search began in Upper West Concocheague Presbyterian Church, Mercersburg, Pennsylvania and this information is used by kind permission of by Mrs. H. Virginia Gress Smith, Mercersburg, Pennsylvania. In 1985 she transferred data from original church records to index cards and subsequently to computer disc in May 2006.[47]

The following information was retrieved:

Marriages performed by John King, D.D. 1769 – 1812 - James Buchanan married Elizabeth Spear (Speer) on 16 April 1788.
This document proved that I had been wrong in my supposition that Elizabeth Speer (Spear) had been married in Lower Marsh Creek church, as her parents had been found buried in the graveyard belonging to that church. However this does confirm the date and place of the marriage and that it actually took place on the 16 April, 1788. However I now understand that the Rev. John King travelled around by horseback and arrangements were made to suit his itinerary. Unless of course that the Lower Marsh Creek church and the Upper West Concocheague were one and the same church?

DEATHS starting 1770 [48]

Buchanan George W. Esq. age 24; 14 Oct 1832 died of consumption
Buchanan child of Jas Buchanan Aug 1801
Buchanan child of Jas. Buchanan 1804
Buchanan James 11 June 1821

These records show:
the death of James Buchanan on the 11 June 1821
the death of two of his children in 1801 and 1804.

Upper West Concocheague Presbyterian Church is now the Presbyterian Church in Mercersburg, which is what the Upper West Concocheague area east of Welsh Run is now called.

I had finally located James Buchanan and Elizabeth Speer and their home at Stony Batter in Cove Gap.

WAS THERE A RECORD OF WHAT LIFE WAS LIKE AT STONY BATTER?

In Mercersburg I searched around for quite some time before I found an amazing answer to this question. The log cabin that had been located at Stony Batter, Cove Gap, had been relocated at Mercersburg Academy grounds for protection against vandals. The reason this had been preserved was because James Buchanan 'the emigrant' had become the father of a President, and this heritage was being preserved for present and future generations to experience.

Illustration 95   James Buchanan's log cabin relocated from Stony Batter, Cove Gap.

Illustration 96   The author at James Buchanan's log cabin in Mercersburg Academy Grounds

Illustration 97   Interior of the log cabin

Philip Klein writes about life in Stony Batter Trading Post. He states that

> 'Stony Batter proved to be a poor place to rear a family. The clearing resounded with the turmoil of stamping horses, drunken drovers, and cursing wagoners.'

He explains that James' wife Elizabeth Buchanan

> 'disliked this raw and uncouth society and lived in constant fear for the safety of her small children who wandered through the ceaseless confusion of horses, wagons, and scattered produce.'

He describes how the business at Stony Batter Trading Post, Cove Gap, prospered and how James Buchanan

> 'was able to buy 'Dunwoodie Farm', in 1794, a splendid 300-acre tract of rich limestone land and timber located about five miles east of Cove Gap, along the West Concocheague Creek, near the village of Mercersburg.' [49]

Illustration 98   Dunwoodie Farm location

Illustration 99   Dunwoodie Farm

Illustration 100   Dunwoodie Farm, Mercersburg - the house has been renamed as 'Patchwork'.

Kline goes on to write that in 1796 James Buchanan

> ' bought a large lot near the centre of Mercersburg and built on it a two-storey brick house to serve both as a home and a place of business.'

His wife was Elizabeth Speer and it was her brother, John Speer, who was put in charge of the Stony Batter Trading Post when James moved to Mercersburg. For the family, life in Mercersburg was 'much more genteel and orderly'.

At that time Mercersburg consisted of nearly a hundred households and this community was almost entirely Scotch and Scotch Irish. As Kline explains

> 'To the Presbyterian Church, one of the oldest in the State, came the Campbells, Wilsons, McClellands, McDowells, Barrs, Findlays, Welshes and Smiths. Buchanan gradually transferred his business to town and soon established himself as one of the leading citizens.' [50]

Illustration 101   Home of James Buchanan, Mercersburg

JAMES BUCHANAN'S FINAL RESTING PLACE

Illustration 102   Spring Grove Cemetery, Mercersburg, founded 1734

Illustration 103   Gravestone of James Buchanan who died 11 June 1821

According to Klein, James Buchanan's death occurred when he was travelling home from Dunwoodie Farm to the house in Mercersburg town. Klein states that

> 'He was just entering the driveway of his Mercersburg home in a rig he had driven from Dunwoodie Farm when the horse bolted, throwing Mr. Buchanan out of the carriage. His head struck the iron tyre, and he died soon thereafter.' [51]

Illustration 104   The family grave of James Buchanan. The smaller gravestones marked his children who had died. In those days the smaller gravestones indicated the young age of the child.

THE INSCRIPTION ON THE GRAVESTONE

This marble covers the remains of
James Buchanan
Who departed this life on the eleventh of July
one thousand eight hundred and twenty one
in the 60th year of his life.
The deceased was a tender husband
and a loving father, and a faithful friend
in all his intercourse with society in which
he maintained the character of an honest man
and a useful citizen. Trusting in the merits
of his Redeemer he entered the dark valley
of the shadow of death expressing an humble
though for him hope of a glorious resurrection.

"Blessed are the dead who die in the Lord".

Transcribed by the author 2008

The family story is that James Buchanan junior resembled his father. The large round eyes are one of the Buchanan traits, and obvious in the photo of Sarah Buchanan of the Carn, Ramelton, alive today. Perhaps this younger likeness of the President gives us some idea of what James Buchanan, the emigrant from Ireland would have looked like.

Illustration 105   James Buchanan, son of James 'the Scotch Irish emigrant'. Courtesy of Franklin and Marshall College Archives

Illustration 106   The sign which is in place at Stony Batter, Cove Gap, Mercersburg

CONCLUSION

The conclusion is that these Buchanan family members in the scroll, which dates back to 1016, did actually exist and prosper. They were like a colony of bees - industrious, adventurous, and prone to migrate and populate. Some overcame tremendous persecution and scarcity. Others died for their faith. Many undertook the journey to the Promised Land in America. Generally, they appeared to be God-fearing people, committed to the life of their church, wherever they moved.

This enabled them, in their mentalités and teleological understanding, to do exploits and live their dreams. They understood that this world was not their home. They lived by their faith. St. Augustine said, 'Faith is to believe what we do not see, and the reward of faith is to see what we believe.' [52] Helen Keller said, 'The only thing that is worse than being blind is having sight but no vision.' The Buchanan family members believed that their vision was to fulfil their God-ordained destiny. However there has to be the acknowledgement that this was not always the case.

In words of James Webb we could say that:

> 'Some continued to marry among themselves, and some did not. Some were wildly prosperous, and some were not. Some cared, some did not. Some remembered pieces of their journey and some did not. Some thought it mattered. Some did not.'

He was answering the question, 'Who are we?' [53] The Buchanan generations past, present and those yet to come are comprised of Ulster-Scots, Scotch-Irish, and Scots-Irish American whose red thread of DNA unravels right back to Anselan O'Cahan who fled from Ulster to Scotland in 1016 and established his family on the east side of Loch Lomond, acquiring the name Buchanan from the lands that they had obtained over the centuries. This is my story.

Illustration 107   Susan and Martha McNutt of Fanad

Illustration 108   Martha was born 1809, married John Buchanan of Garrygort, and was mother of 'White' Sam. She died in 1900 at Garrygort, Milford, age 91 years.

President James Buchanan had visited Ramelton in 1833 on his way back from Russia when he was Ambassador. Cousin John Buchanan and Martha had met him at the party arranged for his visit, and she wrote to him often on the issue of slavery in America after their meeting.

Illustration 109

'White' Sam and Rebecca Buchanan and family, Garrygort, Milford c1900

Back Row: Father 'White' Sam and eldest son, John who inherited Garrygort. Did not marry.

Seated: Mother Rebecca (neé Cheatley) with baby Emily on her knee, Rebecca, Martha, Margaret (Maggie), who was my grandmother

Front row: William Anthony,(joined the Australian Army in WWI)

James David (married Dorothy Stewart, sheep farmer Wylong, NSW, Australia)

Samuel lived and worked in Ramelton

Robert George - Bob – joined Australian Army in WWI, married May Bodley and had 3 sons, Bobby, Keith and Colin.

in adressing this lengthy interrogation to one upon whom I have no claim for the service asked except that of universal and christian fellowship I recognise that I may by its very personal nature be guilty of an imposition I do not for one moment look for nor expect an answer to all the questions proposed but by reason of the great delay in transmission of letters I thought it best to place you at once in possession of the full invitation so that if your knowledge of any of our family's history or the church records should cover any of the points, it would be the more readily grasped at. Your convenience, if you find time to give the matter any attention advising me of the result I will be under many obligations to you.

Later on if you are favored we expect to visit Hamilton when I hope I may have the honour and the pleasure of making your acquaintance

Very Sincerely Yours
James Edward Buchanan
No 610 Augusta St
San Antonio
Texas
U S A

Illustration 110 Our Buchanan reunion at Balmaha, Loch Lomond en route to Clarinch Island 2009.

Alex, Jimmy, Irene, Esther, Robert, Kathy, Eleanor, Keith, Margaret, Jean. (Carol in the blue jacket with a camera was our guide for the day)

Illustration 111 Our Buchanan reunion at Monreagh Ulster-Scots Heritage Centre, County Donegal, May 2010.
Irene, Jean, Margaret, Anne and Eleanor – our great grandfather was 'White' Sam Buchanan of Garrygort, and his father, John, was the cousin of President James Buchanan.

CHAPTER 4   NOTES

[1] Information from *Map location of Carn and Stony Batter,* (2005) Ordnance Survey Ireland 3rd Edition Series 6: Donegal. Scale 1:50 000

[2] Information from Griffiths Valuation of Land OSI 1848, Stony Batter - Ask Ireland online resources.

[3] Information from Griffiths Valuation of Land OSI 1848, Ards Big - Ask Ireland online resources.

[4] Information from Griffiths Valuation of Land OSI 1848, Drumbern - Ask Ireland online resources.

[5] Information from PRONI - Freeholders - Poll Book for Co_ Donegal, 1761-75 PRONI Freeholders Poll Book T808/14999

[6] Information from Griffiths Valuation of Land, Carn Low and Clooney ;1847 - 1864

[7] Information from *Griffiths Valuation of Ireland 1854–1864.*

[8] Information from Griffiths Valuation of Land, occupants of Carn Low 1847 - 1864

[9] Information from PRONI Freeholders Poll Book T808/14999

[10] Information from Griffiths Valuation of Land, occupants of Clooney; 1847 - 1864

[11] This was an oral account from my aunt from which I made these notes.

[12] Ship Advertisement,1783; *Londonderry Journal 28th April 1783* MIC/CMS

[13] Dickson, (1966);98. *Ulster Emigration to Colonial America 1718-1775. Appendix* E. *Reproduced courtesy of the Ulster Historical Foundation*

[14] Ship Advertisement, 1783; *Londonderry Journal 28th April 1783* MIC/CMS

[15] Klein,P. (1962), *James Buchanan,* 1; Pennsylvania University Press

[16] Dickson, R.J.,(1966) *Ulster Emigration to Colonial America 1718-1775,113.* Reproduced courtesy of the Ulster Historical Society, Belfast.

[17] Ibid, 112

[18] Date 14/01/1763 Partial Date Doc. Type SNS Log Document added by LT, 04:08:98., CMS/DATABASE Permission kindly granted by The Belfast Newsletter.

[19] Archive The Central Library, Belfast. Doc. No. 9612093 Date 22/06/1767 Partial Date Doc. Type ADV Log Document added by LT, 03:12:96. Transcript For NEW-YORK in AMERICA, CMS/DATABASE Permission kindly granted by the Belfast Newsletter.

[20] Archive The Central Library, Belfast. Doc. No. 9612093 Date 22/06/1767 *Title Safe Arrival of Passengers Belonging to Ship Providence, at New York.* Source: The Belfast News Letter, 6 January

1769. Archive The Central Library, Belfast. Doc. No. 9412126 Date 04/11/1768 Partial Date Doc. Type NWP Log Document added by LT/JW, 11:12:1994. Transcript Charles-Town, Nov. 4. CMS/DATABASE Permission kindly granted by The Belfast Newsletter.
[21] Source *The Londonderry Journal and General Advertiser, Vol.1 No.90 Frid. April 9, 1775* Archive The Ulster American Folk Park. Doc. No. 9909100 Date 09/04/1773 Partial Date Doc. Type SNS Log Document added by LT, 03:09:99. Transcript LONDONDERRY. Permission kindly granted by The Belfast Newsletter.
[22] Klein, P. (1962), *James Buchanan,* 2
[23] Conestoga Wagon on the old Lancaster Turnpike. From *The Settlement and Growth of Pennsylvania* by Walter Lefferts, Ph.D., c 1925, Franklin Publishing and Supply Company, 102
[24] Pennsylvania Archives, 5th Series. York County; Survey A - 411
[25] Hively, N. (2008), *Map of Adams County from original Pennsylvanian Land Records*
[26] Ibid
[27] http://www.gettysburgpresbyterian.org/history/4.html
[28] http://www.greencastlemuseum.org/Ulsterscots/001/first_settlers.htm
[29] *Buchanan Chart 1.* Compiled by W.N. Wilkins, March 1858, Baltimore, Maryland.
[30] Glenn, T. (1899)*The American Genealogist,* 254 - 259
[31] Ibid, 257
[32] Selected from Original Documents in the Office of the Secretary of the Commonwealth, conformably to Acts of the General Assembly February, 1851 and March 1,1852 commencing 1776. Vol. V,35 Pennsylvania.
[33] First U.S. Census of Pennsylvania, 1790; reprint 1908, 307
[34] Heritage Quest Online Revolutionary War
[35] Pennsylvania Archives 3rd S., Vol. XXIV, York Heritage Trust Library
[36] LAND RECORDS:
www.phmc.state.pa.us/bah/dam/rg/di/r1788WarrantRegisters/r17-88AllCountiesInterface.htm
PATENTS AND WARRANTS from Pennsylvania State Archives, Harrisburg. Samuel Buchanan – Patent Book A-10, page 78 – February 7, 1739. The warrants are found listed by surname and warrant date in the warrant registers on this website
(see: http://www.phmc.state.pa.us/bah/dam/rg/di/r17-88WarrantRegisters/r17-88AllCountiesInterface.htm).
Pennsylvania State Archives, Harrisburg; Record Group 17, Records of the Land Office; Patent Index, A and AA Series, 1684-1781 (series #17.147), as found on the website of the Pennsylvania State Archives, January 2011
(http://www.phmc.state.pa.us/bah/dam/rg/di/r17PatentIndexes/r17-PatentIndexMainInterface.htm). For a detailed listing of the state land records, see the listing for Record Group 17 on the website:
http://www.phmc.state.pa.us/bah/dam/rg/rg17.htm.

[37] Ibid
[38] The Donegal Society, Susquehanna River Valley (2008)
[39] Lower Marsh Creek Presbyterian Church
[40] Lestz, G. (1998) *Lancaster County*, 3
[41] Bloom, R.(1992), *A History of Adams County, Pennsylvania*, 42
[42] Land Grant for Cove Gap to John Tom
http://www.phmc.state.pa.us/bah/dam/rg/di/r17-114
[43] Land Warrant to John Thom (detail) different spelling of surname
http://www.phmc.state.pa.us/bah/dam/rg/di/r17-114
[44] Fendrick,V. *American Revolutionary Soldiers of Franklin County,PA, 5th Series, Volume 6; 272, 285, 315.* The Virginia Shannon Fendrick Library Document Collection, Mercersburg.
[45] Klein,P. (1962); *James Buchanan; A Biography;* 3
[46] Hively,N. *The Chanceford Townships, Chanceford and Lower Chanceford Townships, York County, Pennsylvania:* Original Pennsylvania Land Records (volume 8), 1997
[47] Fendrick Library, Mercersburg;
http://fendricklibrary.home.comcast.net/~fendricklibrary/marriages/
[48] Fendrick Library, Mercersburg
http://fendricklibrary.home.comcast.net/~fendricklibrary/deaths
[49] Klein,P. (1962); *James Buchanan; A Biography*; 4
[50] Ibid;4
[51] Ibid; 37
[52] http://www.ucb.co.uk/3reasons
[53] Webb, James (2009), *Born Fighting. How the Scots-Irish shaped America, 338*

APPENDIX I

An example of early Buchanan marriage networks

Walter Stewart, 6th High Steward of Scotland **m** Elizabeth, daughter of Sir Adam Mure, of Rowallan

John Stewart, Earl of Carrick, b1337 Succeeded to the throne as King Robert III

Walter Stewart (died without issue)

Robert Stewart, first Duke of Albany b1340, Regent of Scotland **m** Isabel, eldest daughter of Duncan, Earl of Lennox

Isobel Stewart m **Sir Walter Buchanan 13th Laird** (born 1415)

APPENDIX II WILLS

Wills and Testament Search Returns

Name	No	Date	Description	Type	Court	Reference
Buchanan John	55	21/11/1617	of Gartincaber	Testimony Dative and Inventory	Glasgow Commissary Court	CC9/7/62
Buchanan John	56	12/08/1617	of Gartincaber	Elk	Glasgow Commissary Court	CC9/7/62
Buchanan John	58	26/11/1616	of Gartincaber Parish of Inschcalleoch	Testimony Dative and Inventory	Glasgow Commissary Court	CC221/5/6

APPENDIX III

The "Killing Times" [1]

According to Dane Love:

'The period from 1680 until 1685 was one of the fiercest in terms of persecution and a few months between 1684-5 became forever known as the "Killing Times". Charles' brother James II had come to the throne, he was a believer in the Divine Right of Kings and a supporter of the Roman Catholic faith. It became his sworn intent to totally eradicate the Presbyterians.' [2]

Presbyterian Covenanters at a Conventicles meeting

'Parish Lists were drawn up in accordance with instructions to the Episcopalian Curates to furnish Nominal Rolls of *all* persons, male and female, over the age of 12 within their Parishes. The Ministers were ordered to give "*...a full and complete Roll of all within the Parish*" and "*that to their Knowledge they give Account of all Disorders and Rebellions, and who are guilty of them, Heritors or others..*" Their instructions concluded, "*No remarks need be made upon these Demands made upon every Curate in every Parish; they are plain enough, as also their Design.*" The 'design' of this census was obviously to assist in the control and persecution of the Covenanters.'

One of the most well known martyrs' resting place is in Hamilton old Kirkyard where there is a tombstone to the 'Heads of John Parker, Gavin Hamilton, James Hamilton and Christopher Strang, who suffered at Edinburgh, 7th December 1666', eight years before George Buchanan emigrated from his home at Blairlusk to Deroran in Ireland in 1674.

---

[1] The Covenanters (2009); http://www.sorbie.net/covenanters.htm
Scottish Covenanter Stories: Tales from the Killing Times by Dane Love
[2] www.covenanter.org.uk

APPENDIX IV

SASINES OF LANDS HELD BY THE BUCHANANS IN SCOTLAND.[1]

Thomas Buchanan, the first of Drummikill, was third son of Sir Walter Buchanan of that Ilk. **1** A charter in his favour, granted by Patrick Buchanan of that Ilk, his brother, of the lands of Gartincaber, to be held blench of the said Patrick, is dated at Buchanan 1461. **2** He had also a charter, dated at "Trefichin," 3rd February 1461-2, of the Temple lands of Letter. **3** On the 2nd of October 1472, Patrick Haloden, bailie for John Halden of Gleneagles, gave sasine to Thomas Buchanan and Robert Makcalpyn of the lands of Ballvol and Camquhele. **4** "11th January 1476-7, campeared Agnes Menteith . . . and gave her oath that she gave her free consent to the sale made by her husband [Haldane of Gleneaglas] of the lands of Kypdory, Carbeth, Ballawoul . . . to Thomas Buchquhhanan of Garcabyr." **5** 1482, the last day of May was made a resignation by Thomas of Buchquhanan of Gartincabir in the hands of a noble man, John Haldane of Glenneaglas, his lord superior, of all and sundry the lands of Carbeth and Ballyvow with the pertinents, which resignation being made, the said lord superior conveyed the said lands of Carbeth to Thomas of Boquhanan, one of the sons of the said Thomas, and the said lands of Ballyvow, with the pertinents, to Walter of Boquhanan, one of the sons of the said Thomas, heritably, according to the tenor of the charter, . . . and conveyed the lands of Kepdory, with the pertinents, to Robert of Bouchquhanan, son and heir apparent of the said Thomas . . . reserving a reasonable third part of all and sundry the said lands, with the pertinents, to *Donata*, spouse of the said Thomas." **6** About 1477 Thomas Buchanan also acquired from the Napiers the Temple lands of Ballikinrain (or Hospital of Innerreith). **7** In 1484 Thomas Buchanan had a charter from William, Lord Graham, of the 40s. lands of Middle Ledlowan (now The Moss), **8** and is therein styled " of Bultoune" (Ballantoun). That Thomas Buchanan of Bultoune was also of Gartincaber is proved by the retour of his descendant, William Buchanan of Drummikill, in 1606, when Thomas is styled "of Gartincaber and Bultoune." **9** He was in possession of Drummikill by 1495, for on 28th February, 1495-6, he resigned one-half of the lands in Favour of Robert Buchanan his son. **10** In 1496 Thomas Buchanan of Drummikill gave sasine to Andrew Cunninghame of the lands of Ardache. **11** That Thomas Buchanan of Gartincaber and Thomas Buchanan of Drummikill were one and the same person is proved by the transaction, quoted further on -- Robert Buchanan, husband of Margaret Hay, being in the Old Protocol Book styled son and heir, in 1472, of Thomas Buchanan of Gartincaber;

---

[1] Footnotes to Chapter XXIII - The Buchanans of Drummikill and Cadets excerpts from *"History of Strathendrick",* pp. 309-310, written by John Guthrie Smith, published by Maclehose and Sons, Glasgow, 1896

and in the Register of the Great Seal the same Robert is in 1515, by which time he had succeeded, styled Robert Buchanan of Drummikill. Thomas Buchanan had at least three sons: (1) Robert, who succeeded him in Drummikill, Moss, and others; (2) Thomas of Carbeth; 12 and Walter of Balwill.

APPENDIX V

MUSTER ROLLS COUNTY DONEGAL 1630
(Names in italics linked to our family tree)

Barony de Rapho
The Lord Duke of Lynox, (Lennox) Scottish Undertaker of 4000 acres, his men and armes

Robert Buchanan
Alexander Buchanan
John Buchanan
John Lowrye
Thomas Lowrye
William Wilson
William Cuthbertson
James Wilson

Note: There were no entries in the muster rolls for the baronies of Kilmacrenan or Tirhugh, both of which remained populated largely by Irish Catholics, although the majority of the land had been granted to English or Scottish undertakers or servitors. Kilmacrenan barony had been reserved for native Irish undertakers, including the MacSweeneys and O'Donnell ruling lines.

Barony de Rapho
Mr. Cahoune Lard of Luce, undertaker of 1,000 acres, his men and armes.

Patrick Buchanan

Barony de Rapho
The Lo: Bpp of Rapho his churchlands being 2,700 acres, his men and armes.

Robert Buchanan
John Wilson

APPENDIX VI

CHURCH OF IRELAND RECORDS
1668 - 1803   PRONI

Church of Ireland, Aughnish or Tullyaughnish,and Tullyfern
(Raphoe Diocese)
Baptisms 1798 -; marriages, 1788 - ; burials
1798 -   MIC/1/167A/1   MIC/1/167A/1

Church of Ireland, Cappagh,   MIC/583/1,
Co Tyrone (Derry Diocese)   27, 30
Baptisms 1753 -; marriages, 1752 - ; burials   T/679/4, 303,
1758 - vestry minutes,1755 -   328

Church of Ireland, Clogher,
Co Tyrone (Clogher Diocese)   MIC/1/22,23
Baptisms 1763 -; marriages, 1777-8, 1796 - ;
burials 1783, 1798 ;
1798 - ; list of churchwardens, 1713 - ; vestry
minutes, 1713- 95

Church of Ireland, Culdaff, Co Donegal (Raphoe
Diocese, formerly Derry)   D/803/1
Baptisms 1668-c1790 (with gaps); marriages,
1713 - 21, 1770-82 ;
burials 1714 - 18 - vestry
minutes,1693-1803

Church of Ireland, Donacavey or
Fintona (Clogher Diocese)   MIC/1/45/2
Vestry minutes, 1779-, including
poor lists, 1783-
Notes on the vestry book, 1778-
1802   D/1048/4

Church of Ireland, Donagheady
(Derry Diocese)   MIC/1/35-36
Baptisms, 1697-1723, 1753-65; marriages,
1697-1726, 1754-64;
burials, 1698-1726, 1754-7; vestry minutes,
1697-1723, 1754-;
confirmation list 1701, poor lists,
1726-38

Church of Ireland, Drumhome, Co Donegal
(Raphoe Diocese)   MIC/1/148
Baptisms, 1719-20, 1739-48, 1764, 1783-;
marriages, 1691-1718,
1764, 1783-; burials, 1696-1715,
1764, 1783-

Church of Ireland, Kilbarron, Co
Donegal (Raphoe Diocese)   MIC/1/156A/1
Baptisms, 1785-93; marriages,
1785-; burials, 1785-

Church of Ireland, Kilcronaghan, Co Donegal
(Raphoe Diocese)   MIC/1/52/1
Baptisms, 1790-; marriages,
1748-;

Church of Ireland, St Eunan's Cathedral, Co
Donegal (Raphoe Diocese)   MIC/1/95/1
Baptisms, 1771-83, marriages,
1771-; burials, 1771 - 83;

vestry minutes, 1673

Church of Ireland, Termonmaguirk, Co Tyrone
(Armagh Diocese)   MIC/1/340D/1

Vestry Book, 1786   CR/1/46/1

Pre-1800 PRESBYTERIAN RECORDS - TYRONE'S
DITCHES
Baptisms, 1793-; marriages,
1794-; stipend collected, 1790-   MIC/1P/457
(the foregoing are all in loose leaf
bundles of pages)

Ballykelly - Baptisms, 1699-1709
(including index);   MIC/1P/208
marriages, 1699 - 1740
(including index)

Information and help in locating these resources acknowledged from

W. L. Roulston in his publication 'Researching Scots-Irish Ancestors'.

APPENDIX VII

FLAX GROWERS LIST 1796   Tyrone and Donegal

Bryans	Richard	Clonfeacle	Tyrone
Bryars	Robert	Aghaloo	Tyrone
Buchanan	Andrew	Termonmaguirk	Tyrone
Buchanan	Bray	Donacavey	Tyrone
Buchanan	Daniel	Donacavey	Tyrone
Buchanan	George	Donacavey	Tyrone
Buchanan	John	Donacavey	Tyrone
Buchanan	Patrick	Longfield East	Tyrone
Buchanan	Robert	Donacavey	Tyrone
Buchanan	William	Donacavey	Tyrone
Buchannan	George	Donaghedy	Tyrone
Buchannan	James	Aghaloo	Tyrone
Buchannan	Patrick	Donacavey	Tyrone
Buchannan	Robert	Leckpatrick	Tyrone
Buchannan	William	Errigal Keerogue	Tyrone
Buchannon	George	Kilskeery	Tyrone
Buchannon	John	Cappagh	Tyrone
Buchannon	John	Drumragh	Tyrone
Buchannon	Joseph	Urney	Tyrone
Buchannon	Robert	Cappagh	Tyrone
Buchannon	Thomas	Kilskeery	Tyrone
Buchannon	William	Clogherny	Tyrone
Buchannon	William	Drumragh	Tyrone

FLAX GROWERS LIST   1796   Co Donegal

Buchannan	Andrew	Donaghmore	Donegal
Buchannan	Daniel	Conwal	Donegal
Buchannan	Francis	Conwal	Donegal
Buchannan	James	Killaghtee	Donegal
Buchannan	James	Kilmacrenan	Donegal
Buchannan	Oliver	Conwal	Donegal
Buchannan	William	Clondavaddog	Donegal
Buchannon	Alexander	Raphoe	Donegal
Buchannon	Finlay	Taughboyne	Donegal
Buchannon	George	Clonleigh	Donegal
Buchannon	James	Taughboyne	Donegal
Buchannon	John	Clonleigh	Donegal
Buchannon	John	Kilmacrenan	Donegal
Buchannon	John	Raphoe	Donegal
Buchannon	John	Tully	Donegal
Buchannon	Philip	Tully	Donegal
Buchannon	Robert	Clonleigh	Donegal
Buchannon	Robert	Kilmacrenan	Donegal
Buchannon	Samuel	Tully	Donegal
Buchannon	Walter	Tully	Donegal
Buchannon	William	Aghanunshin	Donegal
Buchannon	William	Clonleigh	Donegal
Buchannon	William	Conwal	Donegal
Buchannon	Wm.	Raphoe	Donegal

APPENDIX VIII

CIVIL SURVEY 1655 PARISH OF RAPHOE

Thomas Stewart and Robert Buchanan in land arrangements

Source: CIVIL SURVEY 1655 Parish of Raphoe [1]

Robt. Buchanan Brittish ptestt.   Blen mc Quin & Cullachybeg
Mr. Robt. Buchanan gent holdeth ye pmisses by ye like deed of Indenture for ye space of sixty yeares comencing 14th July 1634.

George Buchanan brittish ptestant   An house & garden 4 acres of land & 4 cowes grazing
Parish of Ray
Name of Proprietor   Denomination of Land
The Admrs. of Alexr. Gauthry   Ray (next townland to
Esqr. (viz) Dr. Jon Lesly & Mrs. Clooney and Cairn)

Robt Buchanan brittish ptestts.
The Admrs. of Alexr. Guthry Esqr. holdeth the pmisses by deed of Indenture from Doctr. Jon. Lesly then Bp. of Rapho for the terme of 58 yeares comencing y first of fbr 1636 at the rent as in ye mgent.

Name of Proprietor: Thomas Stewart Esqr. Scotts Protestantt besiedger of Derry
Denomination of Lands: Carrocuilt, Gortcally, Kairne, Clouny, (Garrygort, Cairn and Clooney) where Buchanans were located in 1700.

CONCLUSION from the Civil Survey of 1655

George Buchanan lived at Ray, Ramelton in 1634. This is the adjoining townland to Cairn and Clooney. Thomas Stewart was the proprietor of the adjoining townlands of Cairn and Clooney in 1634. This townland of Cairn – is the migration destination of Thomas Buchanan from Deroran, Co. Tyrone in 1700. This was evidence of most probably a familial information network at work.

---

[1] http://www.ulsterancestry.com/ua-free-CivilSurvey1654.html Parish of Raphoe

APPENDIX IX

No of acres	Undertaker	Dwelling	Freeholders	Lessees	Houses	Cottagers	Men with arms
1. 3,000	Duke of Lennox	a very strong castle, built of lime and stone, but no freeholders	0				The land was well inhabited and full of people. (No Names) (absentee undertaker)
2. 1,000	Sir John Colquhoun, Laird of Luss (transferred from Sir Walter Stewart)	Stone bawn with a poor house	2	3	5	26	This estate was held in 1662 by Hymphrey and Robert Galbraith who sold it back in 1664 to Sir John Colquhoun, son of The Laird of Luss.
3. 1,000	Alexander McAula	Stone house and bawn	2	9		30	
4. 1,000	John Cunningham	Stone house and bawn with houses and water-mill	2	12	26	village of 50	On November 1, 1614, John Cunningham leased several parcels of his land to the following persons: James Robbin, Robert Hunter, John Martin,

William Martin, James Patterson, Alexander McKilchany, John Ploughman, John Molsed, Robert Allane, John Fyeff, Donnell McKilmun, John Wilson, Bernard Coningham, James Boyl, John Bryce, William Sare, Donald Gillaspick, John Fleminge, Donnell McEvene, William McCassack, Alexander Colewell , John Wigton, John Ramsay, Stephen Woolson, Andrew Calwell, William Coningham, Andrew Coningham, Robert Boyl, Donnell Connell. *(Inquisitions of Ulster, Donegal, 5,Car.I.)*

APPENDIX X

HEARTH MONEY ROLLS 1662   PRONI T/307A   Deroran, Tyrone and Taughboyne, Donegal

14th & 15th Chas. II. c. 17 (1662). Imposes a tax of 2s.each on every "hearth and other place used for firing and stoves within every (dwelling and other house and edifices that are or hereafter shall be erected within Kingdom of Ireland other than such as are in this Act hereafter excepted), sec 1. Persons living on alms exempted, sec 13, and all houses certified by two justices to be not of greater value than 8s. upon the full improved rent, and that the persons occupying the same do not have use or occupy any lands or tenements of the value of 8s. per acre, or have any lands, tenements, goods, or chattels of the value of £4 in their own possession, or held in trust for them, sec 14. (Restricted to windows by 17 & 18 Chas. II c 18 sec II (1665).")
17 & 18 Chas. II., c. 18 (1665). Houses having no fixed hearth with chimneys chargeable with two hearths, sec 14.
A return of all the Hearth, Fireplaces, and Stones within the County of Tiron, as the same was returned and taken att a private Sessions held att Newstewart on 28th March in eighteenth year of the raigne of our Soveraigne Lord Charles the Seacond by the Grace of God, of England, Scotland, France and Ireland, King, defend of the faith, &c befor Gerard Jevine, esq., Dr. Thomas Buttolph, and Bernard Buterfield, esq., his Maties Justices of the Peach in the county aforesaid for one year commencing at Michaelmas 1665 and determining at Michms. 1666

HEARTH MONEY ROLL 1666   PRONI T/307A
OMAGH BARRONY Parish of Termonmagork

Denominascons of Lands	Mens Names	Fire Hearths
Deroran	Donaghij Magunshanan	1

For County   (128 Hearths)

Sum Total, £324 16s.

Signed: Tho Buttolph Ger. Frome Tho. Golborne page 315

In 1666 in the townland of Deroran there was only one person named on the Hearth Money Roll. That person was Irish, named Donaghij Magunshanan.

HEARTH MONEY ROLLS 1665

PARISH OF TAUGHBOYNE, BARONY OF RAPHOE

PERSONS WHO PAID HEARTH MONEY TAX IN THE PARISH OF TAUGHBOYNE, BARONY OF RAPHOE, CO. DONEGAL, IRELAND IN 1665.

Indexed by Marianne Philson, Auckland, New Zealand. 25 May 1994.

NAME	TOWNLAND	YEAR
BUCHANAN John	Tullirapp	1663
BUCHANAN John	Clashogowan	1663
BUCHANAN John	Tullyrap	1665
BUCHANAN John	Rusky	1665
BUCHANAN John	Carnsaannagh	1665
BUCHANAN Daniell	Culm'atraine	1665
BUCHANAN John	Taughboyne	1665

Teach Baoithín - Taughboyne

'A parish, in the barony of RAPHOE, county of DONEGAL, and province of ULSTER, 5 miles (W. S. W.) from Londonderry, on the road to Raphoe; containing, with the village and ancient disfranchised borough of St. Johnstown, 6335 inhabitants. St. Baithen, son of Brendan, a disciple and kinsman of St. Columb, and his successor in the abbey of Hy, founded Tegbaothin in Tyrconnell: he flourished towards the close of the sixth century. The parish, according to the Ordnance survey, comprises an area of 15,773 3/4 statute acres, including a large portion of bog: the land is chiefly arable, and of good quality. There are some extensive slate quarries, but the slates are small and of a coarse quality. The river Foyle, which bounds the parish on the east, is navigable for small boats to St. Johnstown, where a fair is held on Nov. 25th.'

(Extract from A Topographical Dictionary Of Ireland by Samuel Lewis, 1837)

There was a John Buchanan who lived just across the Foyle River from the Bready Landing place in 1665. Perhaps this was the link with relatives from the Plantation of Ulster - the Buchanans who were planted on the lands of the Duke of Lennox in this area.

SELECT BIBLIOGRAPHY

Akenson, D. (1996). *The Irish Diaspora: A Primer.* Belfast: The Institute of Irish Studies, Queen's University.

Bruce, M. B. (1995). *The Buchanans:Some Historical Notes.* Stirling: Stirling Council, Libraries Community Services.

Buchanan, W. (1723). *A Historical and Genealogical Essay Upon the Family and Surname of Buchanan.* William Buchanan of Auchmar.

Burke, J. (1835). *A Genealogical and Heraldic History of the Commoners of Great Britain and Ireland.* Colburn, Original in Oxford University, digitalised March 14th 2007.books.google.com/books;p59.

Cullen, L. (1982). The Emergence of Modern Ireland 1600-1900. London: Batsford.

Day. A., McWilliams, P. (eds) 1990,91. *Ordnance Survey Memoirs of Ireland Parishes of County Tyrone 1821, 1823, 1835-36 Vol.5* Belfast: Queen's University.

Day. A., McWilliams, P. (eds) 1993. *Ordnance Survey Memoirs of Ireland Parishes of County Tyrone 1825, 1833-1835,1840 Vol.20* Belfast: Queen's University.

Dickson, R. (1966). *Ulster Emigration to Colonial America 1718-1775.* London: Routledge and Keegan Paul. Reproduced *courtesy of the Ulster Historical Foundation, Belfast.*

Duffy, S. E. (1997). *Atlas of Irish History.* Dublin: Gill & Macmillan.

Fitzgerald, P. (2004). Black '97:Reconsidering Scottish Migration to Ireland in the Seventeenty-Century and the Scotch-Irish in America. In K. A. Young, *Ulster and Scotland.* Dublin: Four Courts Press.

Fitzgerald, P; Lambkin, B. (2008). *Migration in Irish History, 1607 - 2007.* Basington: Palgrave Macmillan.

Gillespie, R. (1991). *The Transformation of the Irish Economy, 1550 - 1700, Studies in Irish Economic and Social History,VI.* Dundalk: The Economic and Social History Society of Ireland.

Gray-Buchanan, A. (1906). *George Buchanan: Glasgow Quatercentenary Studies.* Glasgow: MacLehose & Sons.

Guthrie, J. (1896). *Strathendrick and its inhabitants from early times.* Glasgow: James MacLehose and Sons.

Kelly,W. and Young, J. (2004) *Ulster and Scotland 1600 - 2000.* Dublin: Four Courts Press.

Kenny, K. (2004). *Ireland and The British Empire.* Oxford: Oxford University Press.

Klein, P. (1962), *James Buchanan: A Biography.* Connecticut: American Political Press.

Leiper, J. (2000). *A millenium Account of Drymen and District.* Drymen: Drymen and District Local History Society.

Leiper, J. (2007). *Eleven Large Houses of the Lennox.* Drymen: Drymen and District Local History Society.

Leyburn, J. (1962). *The Scotch Irish; A Social History.* Chapel Hill, NC: University of North Carolina Press.

MacRaild, D. and Taylor, A. (2004) *Social Theory and Social History.* Basingstoke: Palgrave and Macmillan.

McCarthy, A. (2007). 'Bands of Fellowship: the role of Personal Relationships and Social Networks among Irish Migrants in New Zealand, 1861 - 1911. In Enda Delaney and Donald MacRaild, *Irish Migration, Networks and Ethnic Identities Since 1750.* Oxon: Routledge.

McGrew, W. (1998) *Tombstones of the Omey,* Omagh Family History Society.

Mackenzie, G. (2003). 'The De Lanys of Lennies of the Ilk' TSG, Vol. L, No. 1, March 2003. Glasgow: *The Scottish Genealogist.*

McNeill, D. (1964). *The Art and Science of Government among Scots.* Glasgow: MacLellan.

Miller, K. (1985). *Emigrants and Exiles: Ireland and the Irish Exodus to North America.* Oxford: Oxford University Press.

Robinson, P. (1984). *The Plantation of Ulster: British Settlement in an Irish landscape, 1600 - 1670.* Dublin: Gill and Macmillan.

Roulston, W.(2000). 'Ulster Plantation in the manor of Dunnalong 1610-70', in *Dillon, C. and Jefferies, H.A. (ed), Tyrone, History and Society* : Dublin. Geography Publications.

Vann, B. (2008). *In Search of Ulster-Scots Land.* Columbia: University of South Carolina Press.

Webb, J. (2009). *Born Fighting. How the Scots-Irish shaped America.* Edinburgh: Mainstream Publishing Company

Wilson, D. and Spencer, M.(2009). *Ulster Presbyterians in the Atlantic World.* Dublin: Four Courts Press.

Map of Milford, Kilmacrennan and Ramelton family locations in Co. Donegal, Ireland

Lough Natoe

Lough Nacreaght

Lough Donnell

Lough Reelan

Carrownaganonagh

Lough Salt

Gortmacal More

Court

To Kilmacrennan

Skreen Upper

Port

Lough Keel
Ballyscanlon